The Guildry of Dundee

A history of the Merchant Guild of Dundee up to the 19th century

Annette M. Smith

with a Foreword by David Goodfellow, former Lord Dean of Guild

ABERTAY
HISTORICAL
SOCIETY

Number 45

Dundee

2005

ISBN 0 900019 42 5

Printed by Tayport Printers
Tel: (01382) 552381

CONTENTS

LIST OF ILLUSTRATIONS

Main cover image: David, Earl of Huntingdon, as depicted in one of the stained glass windows from the Guildry Room in the Town House (now preserved in McManus Galleries). It was designed by Edward Burne-Jones and executed by William Morris.

Background cover image: A modern copy of the Charter granted by King John of England to the Earl of Huntingdon to enable the Burgesses of Dundee to trade freely throughout all the King's lands except London. Calligraphy by Mr. Donald Shannon.

All images courtesy of Mr. Alexander Coupar except main cover image (McManus Galleries & Museum), plates 1 & 2 (Dundee Central Library, Local Studies department) and 17 (author's photograph)

ABBREVIATIONS

A.P.S.   *Acts of the Parliament of Scotland,*
            eds T. Thomson and C. Innes (12 Vols., 1814-75)

C.R.B.   *Extracts from the Records of the Convention of Royal Burghs,*
            ed. J. Marwick

D.C.A.   Dundee City Archives

D.C.L.   Dundee Central Library.

D.T.C.   Dundee Town Council minutes

E.U.P   Edinburgh University Press

G.   D.C.A; GD/GRW/G Guildry records

HF/M/   Records of the Maltmen Incorporation of Dundee

Lamb.   D.C.L Lamb Collection

N.S.A.   New Statistical Account

S.B.S   Scottish Burgh Survey

S.B.R.S.   Scottish Burgh Records Society

TC/56   D.C.A. copies of Guildry Records in D.T.C. archives

ACKNOWLEDGEMENTS

My grateful thanks must go to the Guildry of Dundee, first for allowing me to use their records in Dundee City Archives, and secondly, on behalf of the Abertay Historical Society as well as for myself, for covering the financial costs of the publication of this volume. Mr. David Goodfellow, a former Lord Dean, has given me so much support and invaluable information, from his vast experience of the Guildry and the Nine Trades, quite apart from his own useful short history, *Guildry of Dundee*. Two other guild brothers have also to be specially thanked for their help. Mr. Dennis F. Collins, the Guildry archivist, is also a mine of information. He and Mr. Alexander Coupar, who has taken the fine photographs of the Guildry artefacts, have been responsible for selecting many of the illustrations, which help to illuminate the activities of the Guildry over the centuries. Mrs. Elspeth Collins too must be thanked for her help in producing the lists of past deans and current guild brothers.

I must also thank the Maltmen Incorporation who gave me permission to read and quote from their records in Dundee City Archive. Mr. Iain Gilroy very kindly allowed me to read his unpublished research, which illuminates Dundee local and national politics in the early nineteenth century.

Everyone who has done any research in Dundee City Archives knows that the cooperation, the tremendous enthusiasm and the deep knowledge of their records, of the two archivists, Iain Flett and Richard Cullen, make research into Dundee history a much simpler business than it might be. My heartfelt thanks go to them and their staff. In the Local Studies Department of Dundee Central Library researchers into Dundee history are also blessed by meeting interested staff who could not have been more helpful when I spent time there.

Dr. William Kenefick and Dr. Alan MacDonald have been sympathetic and perceptive editors. Matthew Jarron, secretary of the society, has been of great assistance, particularly where illustrations are concerned. Finally, I must recognise the contribution to this volume of my son-in-law, David Skett, who so patiently dealt with the worst examples of my inefficiency at the computer.

For all omissions and errors, however, I must be held solely responsible.

Annette M. Smith, July, 2005.

FOREWORD

One hundred and thirty years have passed since Alexander Warden wrote his *Burgh Laws of Dundee* so a new history of the Guildry Incorporation by the well-known and respected historian Dr Annette Smith is very welcome.

This volume completes the trilogy by Dr Smith written from original records of the Trade and Merchant Guilds of Dundee which played such an important role in the life and management of the city for nearly three hundred years.

Much of the influence which was exercised by these bodies over the trade and commerce of the town is now seen as protectionist but in the light of their times they were safeguarding the livelihoods of their members and, should misfortune befall them, supporting their dependents.

Improved communications destroyed the insularity of pre-nineteenth century town life and town walls were rendered obsolete by stronger national governments. However, an appreciation of the importance of the brotherhood among members of these ancient bodies gives us good reason to value today their bonds of common interest.

Throughout a long and distinguished career as a professional historian, Dr Smith has demonstrated her understanding of and feeling for life within Dundee in the sixteenth to nineteenth centuries, and it is with some great delight that this book will allow others to come to an understanding of these important times in Dundee's history.

David Goodfellow, Lord Dean of Guild 1996-1999.

1

THE ORIGINS OF THE GUILDRY INCORPORATION OF DUNDEE

The twelfth century in Western Europe was a period of economic growth in which Scotland shared. A rising population and agricultural prosperity resulted in both the increase in the number of urban centres where traders could meet at markets to sell their surplus produce easily and in the growth of existing settlements. Dundee was one of the oldest settlements in Scotland. With its rich agricultural hinterland, its access to fishing grounds and its favourable location for trading across the North Sea its development had early mirrored that of its counterparts in Europe. In 1199 the burgesses of Dundee were singled out in the English king John's charter signed at Chateau Galliard, Les Andelys in Normandy, which granted them the privilege of free trade throughout all his lands apart from the city of London.[1] This was primarily a favour to John's supporter, Earl David of Huntingdon, brother of William the Lion, but shows that the town was known as a trading post. In 1207 another charter of John's allowing the abbey of Arbroath freedom from tolls when trading with England stated that the Dundee and Perth merchants as the greatest carriers for the abbey were to be under his protection.[2] Another proof of the early commercial importance of Dundee was that while Berwick was the fastest growing trading port in Scotland, Dundee was the only other to have need for a factory for foreign merchants, a privileged group, who assisted their fellow countrymen on visits to the burgh.[3]

Now trade was the mainspring of urban society though not necessarily the only reason for the existence of towns; the merchants whose business was trade tended to become the wealthiest and as a result the most influential members of that society. Within the towns, at an early date, it is possible to find traces of the existence of merchant guilds.[4] Their formal origins are obscure but one certain factor in their formation that can be identified is self-interest. Merchants who traded with other towns, with each other, and with suppliers of goods for sale, recognised at an earlier date than most of their fellow citizens that cooperation was more helpful to their interests than uncontrolled competition, at least among themselves. Restriction of trading activities to a select group and in addition the development of a system of support to all within that group was found to benefit them all.

Early in the history of such associations, members seem to have accepted discipline imposed by the group as a whole, laid out in rules and regulations affecting their business morals and indeed, in some areas, their whole way of life. The head of each individual guild was the dean and members' obedience to his jurisdiction and to the rules of the guild took precedence over all other loyalties, except of course to that of the church. Conflict with town authorities might have arisen but often the ruling bodies of guilds and town councils were in effect the same and worked together, particularly in managing and controlling commercial affairs. Indeed, guilds sometimes initiated formal town government: for instance in Cologne, the committee that managed the merchant guild was also the first formal ruling body of that town.[5] However, one historian of Scottish medieval town life has found little evidence of this happening in Scotland.[6]

Unfortunately, the origins of Dundee Guildry are as obscure as most of those of the town's counterparts on the mainland of Europe. It should be noted that the English king's charter was granted not to any guild or incorporation but to all the burgesses of the burgh. As against that it has been pointed out that merchant and burgess were practically synonymous in early days,[7] but if a guild was in fact in existence at that time it was not as such the recipient of John's favours. A statute of 1209 laid down that merchants of the realm were to have their merchant guild, that each guild was to be content with its own liberty (the area of the burgh itself and any part of its hinterland where the crown might have granted it such privileges) and was not to usurp that of another.[8] A merchant guild in Dundee's rival port, Perth, was granted a charter by the king in the same year,[9] but the Dundee Guild has no proof of having received a similar favour. However, so many of the possible sources of Dundee's history have been lost over the centuries through enemy action, natural disasters and human carelessness that this missing link cannot be taken as proof of anything, positive or negative.

Various suggestions have been made as to when the Guildry was actually founded and it is generally accepted that the Dundee society was one of the first in Scotland. The many contacts that well-travelled Dundee merchants formed with European trading partners must have demonstrated what benefits a guild could bring to its members. A date in the reign of Alexander III, 1249-1286, was suggested by one author,[10] and another historian states categorically that Dundee town council erected its merchant guild in 1249, receiving confirmation by an act of parliament in 1286, but this is difficult to confirm as Dundee City Archive lacks documents for this period.[11] However, this seems to have been accepted as the likely period of its foundation by contemporary historians,[12] though a much earlier date was put forward by a jury appointed by Robert I in 1325 to enquire into the town's privileges.[13] The burgh had appealed to Robert I to secure to them the privileges they believed were theirs by an earlier charter – lost by that time 'if it ever existed'.[14] This jury of burgesses decided that Dundee had enjoyed the privilege of having a guild in the reign of William I, 1165-1214. As a result of their deliberations Robert I's charter of 1327 granted the town all privileges that had existed many years previously, including the right to form a guild of merchants 'as freely as ever our burgesses of Berwick'.[15] It seems highly unlikely that the energetic Dundee merchants would not have seized this opportunity to form their Guildry if indeed they had not done so almost two centuries before. In 1372 an agreement between Montrose guild and that of Dundee by which the two burghs were allowed to trade in each other's district would indicate that there was certainly an active organisation by that time which was recognised by the town authorities.[16] Charles I in 1642 confirmed the Guildry's privileges.[17]

It is only in the early sixteenth century that we have

contemporary local documentary evidence for the existence of the Dundee Guildry. Merchant Guilds were not the only associations of groups with similar interests. Craftsmen too combined to defend their economic strength and to protect their reputation as skilled men. It may have been the actions of Dundee tradesmen that roused the merchants there to the need to obtain legal recognition of what they considered their ancient rights and privileges. In 1503 the Scottish parliament passed an act reaffirming craftsmen's rights,[18] and it has been suggested that this act may also have been a spur to the merchants to approach the council.[19] In 1518, only three years after the Dundee Guildry approached the town council Edinburgh Guildry too applied to its town council for recognition but few other towns in Scotland followed their example at that period and there was never a time when there was a merchant guild in all Scotland's royal burghs.

By the beginning of the sixteenth century several of the Dundee trades had obtained a *'Seal of Cause'* from the town council: a document allowing them to form incorporated bodies with an elected chairman/president, known as their deacon or visitor.[20] Only town councils could make such grants. Alarmed by anything that might erode their rights and established privileges, the merchants took action and on 10 October 1515 they too received the council's official blessing – the Merchants' Letter.[21] In return for supporting a chaplain to the Halie Bluid (Holy Blood) altar in the south aisle of the parish church – who would 'sing and say' divine service daily at the altar and sing mass every Thursday – the 'whole body of the merchants' of the burgh were allowed to elect a dean yearly. This dean was authorised to collect the necessary dues, called the Holy Blood silver, and to exercise the authority of the office according to the laws of the burghs and the *Statutes of the Gild (sic)*. These were statutes drawn up over some years from 1294 in Berwick and were taken as a general example for other burghs, in order to regulate the behaviour of merchants and craftsmen and trade throughout the country and many of the statutes were adopted by the Dundee Guildry. It has been pointed out that other towns might not have had the same pattern of town government as Berwick where the Guildry was dominant but the basic pattern was maintained.[22]

The Merchants' Letter authorised the Dean of Guild to collect taxes from merchants to support and repair the Holy Blood altar, not only on 'this side of the sea' but 'beyond the sea'. Flanders, Zealand, France, Danzig and Denmark were mentioned as well as 'all other parts' where Dundee merchants traded. Cloth, hides and barrels with the dues that could be collected were listed but all goods imported or exported from the town could be taxed, unless the merchants did not think it convenient. In that case the dean or his factor could collect quarterly one penny Scots for each week of the term. The dean and his officers were also given power to seize the goods of any defaulter without any intercession by a law officer. Payment was demanded for privileges such as setting up a booth where goods could be sold. Fines were imposed for any breaches of the rules: for instance a merchant who acted for a person who was not a resident of Dundee would find himself having to pay a fine - money and perhaps wax for candles for the Holy Blood altar. The dean's advice and presence, usually with that of a bailie, though bailies could act alone, was necessary whenever a ship was loaded and no freeman could be made a guild brother without the dean's presence.

James V's charter of 17 July 1526, signed at Edinburgh, confirmed the conditions granted in the Merchants' Letter, but by this time the Dundee Trades had become somewhat alarmed by the extensive nature of the powers the Guildry seemed to have accrued. Many of these were considered to threaten the liberties and privileges some of the Trades themselves had already obtained in their *Seals of Cause*. A further cause of friction was the resentment of the craftsmen at the Guildry's having the sole responsibility for the administration of one of the most important elements of worship in the burgh church.[23]

Relations between the two groups had obviously deteriorated badly and in 1527 it was agreed that formal arbitration was necessary. The Guildry and the Trades each appointed two of their members to choose arbitrators acceptable to both sides: these were Andrew Barrie, a Dundee burgess, and Mr. John Barrie, Vicar of Dundee, to act on behalf of the Guildry; and Mr. George Fernie, chanter of Brechin, and Mr. James Scrymgeour, parson of Glestrie

(Glasterlaw) for the craftsmen. They appeared before the Privy Council in July promising that any agreement made would be adhered to by all parties, and asked to have this recorded in the books of the Council. The arbitrators and all concerned were to meet in the parish church on 1 August under Mr. William Meldrum, dean of Dunkeld, as chairman – then called the 'midman' or 'oversman' – and their final decisions were to be made by the feast of St. Michael. The result was the Decreet Arbitral of 27 September 1527.[24]

The merchants were confirmed in their power to elect a dean of guild who could exercise his authority as it had been 'this 20 yeares bygone': from which it can be assumed that an association of merchants had been in existence before the Merchants' Letter of 1515, though not legally recognised. On the other hand the dean could impose no new statutes or taxes which might damage the craftsmen – 'being brother of the gild'. The town council could, however, cancel any such 'novations', and thus the authority of the dean and his servants to collect dues to support the Holy Blood altar at home and overseas was confirmed. Guild brothers' sons accepted into the Guildry were freed of charges for setting up a booth to sell their goods, fining merchants who acted for non-Dundonians was forbidden, and the dean's presence and advice when ships were freighted was declared unnecessary. Whether this clause was ever effective is unknown, as later records indicate the contrary. There was a further erosion of the powers claimed for the dean in the Merchants' Letter. From 1515 the dean had sole authority to decide whether a merchant was worthy of being made a guild brother or not, but in 1527 arbitrators restored that of the provost and council to be 'used as use and wont' in accordance with the acts and statutes of the town.

Craftsmen were also confirmed in certain powers. Especially, they could once again take legal action against non-residents before their deacons as well as the provost and magistrates. The Merchants' Letter and the craftsmen's letters were to be registered in the common books of the town to ensure that the conditions stipulated therein were adhered to. In addition, the Guildry and all the craftsmen's incorporations were ordered to subject their accounts for annual inspection by the town council; however this was as often ignored as obeyed.

These documents demonstrate clearly that the merchants of the Guildry had been acting together from early in the sixteenth century. A claim for the greater longevity of the incorporation was made in 1606 when it was noted in the minutes that it had been in existence for at least '200 yeares bygone': a century before the Merchants' Letter was written.[25] This date may have been corroborated by some of the Guildry's own records, but these are not now available to us. Without any such evidence we are dependent only on folk memory and oral traditions – unfortunately not always a reliable guide with regard to dates. After 1515, however, the Guildry undoubtedly existed and acted as a recognised and authorised if not an incorporated body. In one of the Protocol Books of the council, that for 1518-1534, the dean of guild appears as a member of the town council in 1526 and was to remain so *ex officio* – with only a short gap in the nineteenth century[26] – until local government in Scotland was completely reorganised in 1975.[27]

It is unfortunate that the original Merchants' Letter seems to have disappeared. It is possible that it was burned in the 1911 fire in the town house which damaged many of the Guildry's records.[28] In 1570 the Guildry began a new book in which were recorded all their activities, rules and regulations and their accounts. One of the first entries after the title page of this – *The Gildrie Book* – was a copy of the letter, the following charter and the decreet arbitral.[29] Only a copy of the actual Letter, made in the early nineteenth century, remains in the town's archive. The document, or a copy or that in the 1570 book itself, came to light in the Guildry's archive in 1815 when the society was struggling to obtain its freedom from dominance by the town council. They were searching for historical proof of their origins and rights and this was a vital weapon in their struggle.

The Gildrie Book is the earliest existing record of the Guildry's proceedings made by the incorporation itself. It is a leather bound volume, initially kept closed under a padlock and key. Most trade and professional incorporations and societies recorded their important private business and their trade secrets in just such a volume – their Locked Book – and the key was placed in charge of the officials of the association. In 1852, the sederunt book of the Guildry was still kept locked and in that year a new lock and key were made – a gift from Mr. William Middleton. The first minute is dated 13 October 1570 and on that day Alexander Scrymgeour was 'elected and chosen' dean by the provost, bailies, council and 'the whole bodie of the merchants and brethren of the gild'. Scrymgeour accepted his appointment and gave his oath that he would carry out his office 'as god sall give him grace'.

This is not the first entry, however, and this volume is not as old as it seems to be at first glance. The records of many years are written in the same hand and must have been copied from an earlier Locked Book, which was then being replaced and like the Merchants' Letter it seems to have disappeared. In 1607 among the 'evidents' (documents and artefacts) the incoming dean received from his predecessor, there were included a 'locked gild book' and 'the present book' and another book described as containing 'the laws of the gild'.[30] Despite each dean's promise to hand on to his successor everything he had received on taking office, there is a definite lack of continuity in the deans' lists and it is difficult to know just which books were meant in that particular list. If one volume was kept solely for recording the Guildry's laws then it too seems to have disappeared. New books were regularly purchased as the need arose when any in use became full or were in poor condition: for instance, the 1649-59 accounts show that £6 was spent a on new book, bought in Holland. Earlier volumes may have been discarded once the copying was done and either lost or destroyed like so many other parts of Dundee's historical archive.

On the back of the title page of the *Gildrie Book*, there is a list of artefacts belonging to the Guildry in the dean's possession, which the current officer would need to carry out his duties. These include for example the weights and measures against which those of merchants would be tested, (see plates 9-12), thus making sure that all goods were fairly weighed; this was one of the responsibilities of the Guildry. The book opens formally with a short list of the acts which refer to merchants' privileges copied out of *Regiam Majestatem*, a collection of medieval Scots law. A few acts of burgh law follow including the rule that no burgess was to deal except in his own burgh. Then, most importantly, are copies of the Merchants' Letter, the charter confirming it in 1526, and the Decreet Arbitral of the following year.

Thereafter the normal business of the dean and his officers including their accounts for many years is recorded over 59 sheets of paper numbered on one side only as folios, until 1641. The next sheet is entitled 'Gildrie Book of Dundee' and from ff.61-76 there are lists of members who have paid their dues, but not in correct chronological order (for example, the first is 1633 but there are earlier entries from 1597, following others for 1609 and some from 1654 are included in ff.90-93). It is not unusual to find such lack of order in older records, particularly if they have been rebound, as has happened to this volume. The accounts for the use and repair of mortcloths, the cloths hired out to members and their families to cover coffins before burial, are included, followed by a few blank pages and then we find the records from 1648-96 (which actually began at the back of the book). As well as confusion in dating, the rebinding has resulted also in some loss of legibility at the end of lines, and particularly so in the earlier folios. Clerks in earlier times often made entries in what may seem to us a somewhat unorthodox manner.

Protection of the privileges and liberties of the Guildry was its main business and this is reflected in the prominence of such subjects in the records. The area of the burgh over which the Guildry's authority held sway was in fact quite small, covering only the original regality or royalty, and this was never extended to the suburbs of the burgh.[31] The great town church of St. Mary was originally the 'kirk in the fields' outside the burgh bounds and the shore line lay much further north. Over the centuries much land has been reclaimed from the Tay but until the nineteenth century, the harbour was only a short distance away from the Marketgait, now the High Street. The town's plan has been described as that of a man lying with his limbs stretched out, the High Street the body, with the four streets Murraygait and Seagait to the east, Flukergait (now

Nethergate) and Argyllgait (now Overgate) the legs and arms. The same basic plan can still be seen today though street levels are higher. In 1819 the only additional districts were the Shore, the Cowgait and the Wellgait.[32]

The royal burghs, originally those founded by the monarch, were alone among Scottish burghs in being allowed to take part in export and import trade until the late seventeenth century. They were also granted power to control trade in the countryside around them, referred to as their 'liberties'. The downside of having such privileges was that they shared in paying taxes, known as cess, although that did obtain the burgh a place in parliament. Dundee had had the status of a royal burgh from the twelfth century, and the burgh's position as an entrepot for goods coming in from the rich agricultural area to its north was strengthened by Robert I's charter of 1327 and David II's of 1359. These allowed only Dundee burgesses to buy wool and skins and Dundee burgesses alone within the sheriffdom of Forfar could trade with foreign merchants. Also various villages such as Coupar Angus were prohibited from holding markets as they were within the liberties of Dundee.

The defence of these privileges was a never-ending struggle for the burgesses and Guildry for many centuries. Obtaining recognition from king, parliament and town council was only the beginning. Within the burgh, they had constantly to be on the watch for what were referred to as 'encroachments' on these liberties and privileges (not only from outsiders) until the nineteenth century. The monopoly on foreign trade was weakened in the seventeenth century, but it was not until 1846 that the monopolistic privileges of royal burghs, and of the incorporations within them fell, before the onslaught of free trade and increasing democracy, following an Act of Parliament which removed the unique historic status of both.[33] The history of the Guildry is the story of how they defended their rights and privileges - legal until 1846 - and how they adapted thereafter to their loss.

NOTES

[1] DCA;1/1 A copy of this charter.

[2] E.P.D. Torrie, *Medieval Dundee* (Dundee, 1990), 31.

[3] A.M. Duncan 'Burghs before 1296', in P. McNeill and A. A.M. Duncan (eds.), *An Historical Atlas of Scotland* (St. Andrews, 1975), 32.

[4] C. Gross, *The Gild Merchant* (Oxford, 1890), 8.

[5] A. Black, *Guilds and Civil Societies in European Political Thought from the Twelfth Century to the Present* (London, 1984), 55 ff.

[6] E. Ewan, *Town Life in Fourteenth Century Scotland* (Edinburgh, 1990), 60.

[7] Torrie, *Medieval Dundee*, 34.

[8] *APS*, i, 61.

[9] M..Stavert (ed.), *Perth Guildry Book, 1452-1601*, (S.R.S 19, Edinburgh, 1993), iv.

[10] Gross, *Merchant Gild*, i, 204

[11] D.B. Morris, *The Stirling Merchant Gild and Life of John Cowane* (Stirling, 1919), 51.

[12] P.G.B. McNeill and H.L. MacQueen (eds.), *Atlas of Scottish History to 1707* (Edinburgh, 1996), 215.

[13] Anon. Review of *The Gild Merchant*, in *Scottish Review*, 1898, 32, 71.

[14] Torrie, *Medieval Dundee*, 23.

[15] W. Hay (ed.), *Charters, Writs and Public Documents of the Royal Burgh of Dundee* (Dundee, 1880), no.16, p..9.

[16] W.M. Mackenzie, *The Scottish Burghs* (Edinburgh, 1949), 103. His source was *Historical MSS*. ii, 206.

[17] Hay, *Charters*, 75.

[18] *APS*, ii, c.29.

[19] D. Goodfellow, *A Brief History of the Guildry* (1997), iii.

[20] A.M. Smith, *The Three United Trades of Dundee* (Dundee, 1987) and *The Nine Trades of Dundee* (Dundee, 1995).

[21] DCA, (Dundee Guildry Record – call papers GD/GRW/G);G1/1, ff.1-4.

[22] Ewan, *Town Life*, 59.

[23] I.E.F.Flett, 'The conflict of the Reformation and Democracy in the Geneva of Scotland' (Unpublished MPhil thesis, St. Andrews University, 1981), 15.

[24] DCA; G1/1, ff.3,4; these documents can be found fairly fully if not 100% accurately in A.J. Warden, *Burgh Laws of Dundee* (London, 1872), 93-101.

[25] DCA; G1/1, f.38 10-2-1606.

[26] See Chap. 3.

[27] W. Wyllie, 'The Guildry Incorporation of Dundee' (Unpublished typescript in Dundee City Archive, n.d.), 1.

[28] Mr. David Goodfellow informed me that the present archivist of the Guildry suggested this solution to the puzzle of its disappearance.

[29] DCA; G1/1, ff.1-4.

[30] DCA; G/1, f.38.

[31] A.M. Jackson, *Glasgow Dean of Guild Court* (Glasgow, 1983), 116.

[32] DCA; G1/5, 30-9-1819.

[33] 9 Vic. C.17.

2

MEMBERSHIP OF THE GUILDRY

The Guildry was founded basically as a society of merchants meeting together to defend their own interests. But who were the merchants? Craftsmen made and sold only their own goods. Merchants on the other hand made nothing but bought and sold goods wholesale, and also sometimes carried on retail business in their booths in the market-place, or even from their own homes. In the royal burghs which had the monopoly of foreign trade at least in theory until 1672, the merchants controlled all such trade. A good many were men of some substance who were able to bulk buy goods, but it has to be remembered that in Scotland the word 'merchant' can refer to any shopkeeper and particularly grocers. In 1580 there were just over ninety names noted as attending one meeting of the Guildry and considering the size of the town it is unlikely that they were all men of great wealth.[1] As one historian has pointed out, most merchants were not international traders but mere stall holders.[2] However, they were still considered as being under the Guildry's authority and this was exercised over anyone, male or female, who tried to make a living by opening a shop until the nineteenth century. In the ancient royalty those who would not, or could not for financial reasons, enter the incorporation were compelled to pay a licence or face court action.

Of course, those who backed such risky ventures as sending goods across the sea to far away places such as the Baltic, the Bay of Biscay, and the Mediterranean needed considerable resources. These areas were familiar to many Scottish traders in the sixteenth century and before. Even though ships did not usually sail in the winter months, the seas were always dangerous to the small vessels of medieval and early modern times. Losses were common and merchants had to be able to bear that risk. In 1529, the Convention of

Royal Burghs laid down that no chapman – a travelling salesman – could become a burgess unless he could show that he had capital of £100 (a very large sum at the time)[3] and as only burgesses, freemen of the burgh, could officially become merchants this was another way of ensuring that only the well-off could enter their ranks.

No matter where they operated burgh merchants clearly had a high opinion of their place and status. For example, in 1590 the Dundee Guild reacted strongly to complaints that members were selling such things as eggs, kail, onions, apples and pears and 'uther like hockstrie form of trade' at their booth doors, and that this was a 'great dishonour of their estate publickly'. Hucksters were traders in small goods, mere pedlars carrying their goods on their backs. The dean and his assessors forbade merchants to take part in such trade from then and laid down penalties of 20s for the first offence, and for any further offence a merchant could risk seeing his shop being closed with a subsequent loss of his privileges. The Glasgow Guild, which obtained its Letter of Guildry in 1605, decreed in a rather contemptuous manner that it was 'not agreeable to the honour of guild brethren to tap (retail) or sell in smalls' – defined in a list similar to Dundee's – or deal in 'the goods that any huckster might bring to market'. Their members were to have the monopoly of expensive goods like silk, spices, wines, foreign hats – most Scotsmen wore bonnets – and alone could buy such goods as salmon.[4]

In the hierarchal society of these earlier days, there was also great attention paid to appearances and to suitable behaviour. Sumptuary laws were passed by the Three Estates, one in 1567 laying down that no woman was to dress above her station – except whores. Dundee town council had decreed that no merchant unless a bailie or 'a worthy man of the council' should wear silk or costly scarlet gowns.[5] Women were warned that they must wear only short curches, head-coverings, and furs were allowed only on holidays: though there seemed to be no restriction on jewellery, one adornment of their wives by which a merchant's wealth could be displayed conspicuously.[6] The Guildry itself in 1588 made its own rules about dress and behaviour. The estate of merchants was told that it should take care to dress in 'honest abuliement of their persons' and in comely behaviour. Such 'honestie' was defined as abstaining from wearing plaids or blue bonnets (the most commonly used): merchants were to sport only black. They should also refrain from pushing barrows around or doing any like labour, at least within the liberties of the burgh. Presumably outside the town the dignity of the Guildry would not be impaired if such actions were not actually seen by the commonality of Dundee. To demonstrate how important it was to keep up appearances and that clothes and manners mattered, merchants found breaking the rules were fined 13s 4d for a first offence, 40s for a second and £10 for the third.[7]

Craftsmen could aspire successfully to becoming guild brethren but in most towns this was possible only if they gave up personal practice of their trade. They could maintain their business only by employing servants, and litsters (dyers) and fleshers (butchers) were singled out in the *Statutes of the Gild* as being totally forbidden entrance as their discoloured hands and clothes always betrayed their calling. However, this veto did not last and by 1570 the Dundee Guildry allowed any member of these trades to become a guild brother so long as he employed servants and did not 'do the craft with his own proper hands'.[8] In 1661-2 entry fees were paid by maltmen, a fishmonger, a glover, a barber, a tailor, a hammerman, a bonnetmaker, a cordiner and a weaver. This seems to show that some craftsmen at least were comfortably off,[9] despite the entry made in 1654 complaining of the 'great decay of men and traid within the burgh'. In an attempt to improve the economy of the burgh, it was decided to encourage 'strangers and traders' – strangers being anyone who was not a resident of Dundee – to come and live in the town by allowing them to become burgesses and practise the merchant trade for the total sum of 40 merks without paying any additional sums such as the booking fee usually paid to the clerk.[10] This incidentally shows how the Guildry were prepared to adjust their rules to suit economic circumstances.

The merchants ranked highest in the social scale in the burgh. Of course, country gentry and aristocrats could have town houses and be residents, but among simple burgesses the merchant was supreme. Indeed, Dundee claimed precedence over Perth in the ranking of Scottish burghs because Perth town council counted such a high proportion of craftsmen among its members. The richest merchants were the wealthiest group and the most influential because of their potential to be members of the town council and because of their vital position in the economy of a burgh so dependent on trade. They stood high in their own estimation and would no doubt have agreed heartily with Daniel Defoe's comment after he had visited Dundee – that 'true bred merchants are the best of gentlemen'.[11]

Wealth is however relative. For example the fact that few of the early deans in the sixteenth century have their testaments recorded in the Commissariot Record of Brechin may indicate that their estates were not large.[12] Further, it was rare for a ship to have only one Dundee merchant's goods in its hold. It has also been pointed out that while the merchants were liable for 40% of the taxation of the burgh in 1588, the assessment fell in that decade, when all the Scottish ports were suffering from the growth of Leith. All the indications are that most of the Dundee merchants at that time at least were comfortably off rather than very rich.[13]

One of the conditions of membership, that guild brethren must also be burgesses, meant that they could trade only in their own burgh. In 1578 a meeting of the Convention of Royal Burghs in Edinburgh, faced with the contravention of this rule by so many freemen of various burghs, decided that only those with permanent dwelling places in a burgh, doing their ward duty and paying taxation, were to be admitted freemen in future. They were given forty days to return to their own burgh under threat of losing their status as freemen both within Scotland and abroad.[14] This would have meant that they could not have become guild members. How effective this ruling was can be judged by how often it or similar ordinances were repeated. In 1621, Dundee, Haddington and Wigtown were asked to show that they were making sure their burgesses did in fact reside in their burghs. In 1694, the Dundee head court warned the Guildry, and the Trades, that they must not admit members without proof of residency.[15] In 1723, Dundee reported to the Convention that they had taken action against 'outland' burgesses, but in 1730 the Guildry reinterpreted the rule to define residency as a freeman as staying with their families in the town for eight months in the year.[16] In light of that rule one man who moved to Arbroath and asked for the return of his bill for £100 Scots – his promise to pay – must have felt rather hardly done by when the collector was ordered to take legal steps to recover the money.[17]

Dundee burgh laws followed those of the Scottish parliaments generally on the question of who could share in the import/export trade, but there seem to be ambiguities in the Guildry's own regulations on entrance. In 1570, at the end of the copy of the arbitration of 1527, a list of duties or fees to be paid to join included two grades, one for freemen and one for the unfree. There was considerable difference in some of these: for wine and wax 10s for the free, 20s for the unfree; 20s to the clerk for writing new members' names in the Locked Book for the free, 26s 8d for the unfree. Permission to practise 'packing and peiling' (buying and selling), cost each the same, 6s 8d. Wine and wax were part of the payment for the upkeep of the altar in St. Mary's church, arranged in the Merchants' Letter in 1515, but of course disappeared from the fees for entry paid after the Reformation (although without the records it is impossible to say exactly when this happened).[18]

It would ordinarily be expected that the 'unfree' were men who were not burgesses, and in theory could not be merchants at all. Therefore the question must arise – did 'unfree' in this context refer only to those merchants who did not enter the Guildry? The town council did not provide a statute until 1720 that no one could trade or keep a shop in Dundee unless he first entered the Guildry, on pain of being fined £100 Scots and lying in prison until this was paid.[19] It was claimed then that the Guildry, not the town it should be noted, was imposed upon by those who came into the burgh to trade without the privilege to do so. However, it seems that the practice of admitting unqualified persons when it suited either body was not unusual or new and regulations in 1593 demonstrate that both the Guildry and the town council had been ignoring their own rules. It was thought that great harm had been done by admitting the unfree in great numbers to be burgesses and brothers of guild and, significantly, 'persons not qualified to use the trade of merchandrie'. In an attempt to remedy the situation it was decided that in future there was to be no entry to the Guild except by those whose 'religion, honestie, conversation and good manners be tried and found worthy of that place and calling'. The further condition that entrants must pay the thesaurer (the treasurer) of the burgh – not the Guildry collector – £40 Scots plus accidents (the term used to cover payment to the clerk and officer) and the fee for packing and peiling (trading generally) certainly ensured that they were men of some considerable means.[20]

No suggestion was made in this description of the skills necessary for acting as a merchant that he should have served an apprenticeship. Throughout most of its history the Dundee Guildry demonstrates some laxity in ensuring that records were kept of its members having been properly trained as indentured apprentices to qualified merchants. Master merchants is not a term that appeared in earlier records, nor was any demand made that a would-be merchant should demonstrate his ability in the same manner as a craftsmen did when producing his masterpiece. In the earliest part of the archive available to us, no reference is made to apprentices. No separate official record of apprentices's names, dues paid, or dates of entering service with a master is to be found in the Guildry's archive, and only occasionally was there any attempt made to obtain any information about prospective members. For instance in 1578 it was decided that no-one could be entered in the Locked Book until he was twenty-one and that the son of any extranear (foreign) burgess could not be accepted as he could not understand the oath.[21]

One unfortunate effect of this lack of information is the impossibility of making any assumptions about the social classes who indentured their sons to merchants in Dundee, nor of the geographical area of their origins, as has been done in other Scottish burghs.[22] The Dundee Trades kept more careful, though not perfect records of their apprentices' antecedents – class background and geographical area of origin for example. The Dundee merchants may have recruited their apprentices similarly, but unfortunately this cannot be proved. The total lack of such information in the Guildry's records is puzzling.[23]

The town council did show some interest in apprenticeship when attempts were made to regulate entry to both town and Guildry. In 1611 there was concern that strangers were coming into the town who had not served as free apprentices and yet were allowed in on the easier conditions granted to these, so a payment of 100 merks was demanded, and apprentices were to register in the town's books.[24] A century later on 24 January 1710 the town council decreed that a book should be made for entering all apprentices of merchants, surgeons, apothecaries, seamen and maltmen (£4 was to be paid to the Guildry and the maltmen were to pay £2). If this book was ever opened it does not now appear in the council's archive. In 1722 a committee, considering the position of apprentices, recommended that all those becoming indentured to the same group as those included in the town council's list of 1710, who were not the children of free guild brothers, should pay £3 Scots to the dean of guild or to the collector for the use of the Guild and 20s Scots at the start of their apprenticeship. Without the mark in the Guildry Book no benefit would be given either to future or present apprentices. It was also suggested that in future anyone taking an apprentice should pay 10s sterling – which incidentally shows that the use of sterling money after the 1707 union of the parliaments was creeping in.[25] Whether these recommendations were approved is uncertain but the inclusion of any other than merchant and maltmen apprentices does not appear to have been carried out.

Complaints are made about different types of irregularities on various occasions. In March 1729 it was alleged that merchants were taking apprentices for one year or 'other short space' in their service. The apprentice then later claimed the freedom of the Guildry for only £5 on the grounds that he was a free apprentice, that is one who had served a full apprenticeship with a free master. Free apprentices would have paid larger dues to the merchant, but then benefited from paying less to become a guild brother. The meeting enacted that three years at least must be served.[26]

Later that year there was still some discomfort with the position of entry generally and a Dean of Guild Court met to consider the effects on the Guildry. More rigid rules were drawn up and the reasons for the disquiet were revealed.[27] The Guildry's financial position was affected in two ways when cheap and easy entry was allowed. Obviously smaller entry fees made for a decrease in the funds generally, but the worried guild brothers pointed out another serious grievance. It was felt that the 'smallness of the dues', less than was asked for entry to the Nine Trades, encouraged inexperienced people to set up shops, including many who were neither free burgesses nor members of the Guildry (perhaps hardly surprising as even today there is a questionable belief that it is easy to run a shop). In addition, lack of proper training of members who had either served too short apprenticeships, or had served merchants who were not themselves necessarily properly trained, led to so-called merchants having no real knowledge of merchandise or stock. This caused many to 'break' and such bankruptcies put an extra burden on the town and the Guildry's poor funds. As the Guildry did try to provide help for sick or poor members this was important for their funds had to be maintained at a level that would enable them to give relief to needy members.

After hearing this argument the Court decided that in future a five-year apprenticeship must be served: indentures must be signed in the presence of the dean; £100 Scots entry money should be asked to cover all dues (which included a fee to the clerk for inserting the names into the Guildry Book), and the sum paid for 'upsetting of booths' when the newly qualified did finally open his shop. No unfree were to be allowed to open shops without the authority of the Guildry Court and after 2 February 1730 offenders would be fined £12 Scots for the first offence, increasing to £24 for a second, with a third costing them £60.

The five-year rule was not always rigidly adhered to even after this. In June 1739 James Nairn requested permission to enter as a free apprentice. His master, Frederick Corsar, had died when Nairn had served only about four years and he felt he needed the authority of the Court to enter. Such respect always had its effect and he was admitted as a full member once he had paid his dues.[28] On the other hand when one master applied for permission for his apprentice to improve his position by becoming a free apprentice, this was refused on the grounds that the master had not applied within the time allowed for making such a change.[29]

Despite any rules made records were rarely complete. Individual apprentices are often mentioned in later years but it would appear that it was up to each of them and his master to ensure the safe-keeping of all the documents needed to obtain entry to the full privileges of the Guildry. The importance of keeping a check on numbers and training is obvious and much depended on the officials in charge at any time, as well as on the actions of the masters and boys involved. Even when professional clerks were employed the competence and energy of these officers could vary considerably. When in the late eighteenth and early nineteenth centuries members numbered over 300 – and were not in fact all active merchants, as that term had been understood initially – it is not surprising that records of apprentices fell by the wayside. However, in 1818 a general meeting of the Guildry trying to regulate entry decided that an apprentice must pay 7s 6d to the clerk for recording his indenture over and above the same sum due when they received entry tickets to the Guildry.[30] But there are still no official records of apprentices to be found. It is also interesting that at one point indentures of surgeons and apothecaries were not accepted as proof that they could share the liberties of the Guildry.[31]

The subject of small shops opening in the burgh also introduces the position of women as merchants. In the changing economy of the eighteenth century, as the population of towns increased, so too did the need for more outlets for retail trade, as food and clothing had to be bought, not grown or made at home. It was often women who tried to make a living by opening a small shop – though this was strictly illegal – and the profit made was rarely enough to pay Guildry dues in many cases. This was not just a problem for the Dundee Guildry. All over Scotland at this time the number of small shops was increasing.[32] Such a clear breach of their rules could not be ignored, so in 1722 the local solution was that young women and widows who set up shops were to be charged 40 merks, if they could afford this, for which they and their children would be free of the Guildry, 20 merks if they could not, which would allow them only to open their shop. This cannot have had much effect for by 1728 only a small licence fee of two to four merks was asked for, but then, feeling that their privileges were 'much encroached on', the Guildry restricted this permission to widows and daughters of guild members.[34]

Though only those who tried to trade in the original royalty were affected by Guildry rules, this area was the commercial centre of the expanding town and therefore more attractive than the suburbs to would-be shopkeepers. In the nineteenth century, until the abolition of all privileges in 1846, there was a concerted effort to control the opening of shops. In March 1818 when the collector reported that several people had opened shops in the Wellgate he was instructed to inform all involved that they must pay dues.[35] The scale of the problem for the incorporation is realised when in the following year forty shopkeepers were asked to join the Guildry or risk being prosecuted.[36] A month later they were told they must pay 40s per year or entry the Guildry free - which seems an odd sort of compromise - but many refused to do either.

The unusual feature of this particular situation was that several women were included among those who received these letters. There did not appear to have been any discussion regarding the possibility of women asking for membership, nor any suggestion that they were not eligible. One woman, Marjorie Scrymgeour, was given the freedom of 'occupation of' the Guildry by the town council in 1552 as a favour to the queen's master of Works, Master John Scrymgeour of the Myris, for 'gratitude done be him to this burgh'.[37] Another woman's name, Miss Jane Pringle, appears in the 1805-06 accounts as having paid the same amount as a man would have for her freedom as a life member – £4 3s 4d.[38] Women did in fact trade, and had to obey the same rules as men such as having to maintain correct weights. Most may have paid only for upsetting their booths, but as women did not ordinarily become burgesses – who in theory alone could share the privileges of the burgh – their legal position may have been precarious.

Within the burgh the sons and sons-in-law of guild brethren were automatically allowed entry on reduced fees. This was such a bonus that there is no doubt that attempts were made to claim membership on very dubious grounds and throughout the records we find the Guildry on the watch to prevent such abuse of their privileges. In 1590 it was believed that a great number of burgesses' sons were claiming all their parents' privileges though there was no proof of their having been received into the society or of having paid any dues. The officers of the Guildry were ordered to collect all the ordinary duties within a month or the offenders would lose for ever any rights they could actually claim through their parents.[39] There was a concession to the Nine Trades in 1713. The town council reported that the Trades had agreed to give any guild brother who married a freemaster's daughter the freedom of her father's trade, and the Guildry reciprocated by offering privileges to tradesmen who became the sons-in-law of guild brothers 'as far as her father enjoyed or had rights' - which was perhaps a significant qualification.[40]

Another threat to the Guildry was posed by the fact that nobles and 'other gentlemen' had been made burgesses by an act of the Privy Council. Their servants could also act as merchants and ordinary burgesses and this too deprived both the town and Guildry of funds. A way to make up this loss was found – these men had to pay double the usual sum for upsetting their booths – four score merks.[41]

In the eighteenth century a new category of entry began to appear. Some entrants paid for privileges for only their lifetime and not for their posterity. This meant that their sons and daughters had no rights to easier entry for themselves or their husbands and no access to poor relief. The benefit to the individual was that he obtained the right to trade and to open a shop without any risk of being harassed by Guildry officers. As entry fees increased, this must have allowed many Dundee traders to aspire to membership with its corresponding privileges at a time when hitherto they could not have considered it. Indeed their fees increased the Guildry's funds without increasing obligations to the individuals concerned. It was always possible for a life member to become a full member by paying the full dues. David Farquharson had paid his lifetime dues in 1790, but in

1825 became a full member, paying the additional sum to make up his fee to £15 16s 8d from the £4 3s 4d – the sum requested for life membership – plus all the ordinary dues to the clerk and the officer. It is probably significant that the same day his two sons were also admitted for £2 10s as offspring of a guild brother and the difference between the two sums made the father's extra expense well worthwhile for all the family.[42] There had been some suggestion about this time to abolish the lifetime entry but the Guildry has still such members.[43]

In the eighteenth century some aspiring members used what might be called a type of hire-purchase entry when the fees increased. In 1700, for example, 100 merks which was equally divided between their burgess fee and entrance to the Guildry, was more than many could raise or perhaps were willing to pay to the collector at one time. Instead they offered bills for the whole, which were a promise to pay at some time in the future (unspecified) and they were granted the liberty of membership at once. This had its difficulties. In 1741, James Anderson, who had not yet paid cash, requested that he should be given his bills back as he had now married Janet Jobson, whose father was a litster and guild brother. This request was granted but a committee was appointed to consider how to avoid the repetition of such practice. What the committee recommended does not seem to have been recorded, but one can understand the worries of the collector if many merchants obtained entrance by such means.[44] Another method of payment was offered by Patrick Cocks. The dean's court authorised the collector to take the right to the rents of Cocks' land for £20 Scots per annum until he had paid the £100 Scots due for his freedom. And as Cocks was to keep the 'writings' – the agreement made – his self-interest was probably more likely to ensure the safety of the contract than leaving it in the hands of the Guildry.[45]

The collector's job was not always an easy one. From the sixteenth to the nineteenth century these officers had to try to extract fees from unwilling payers. In 1590, one complained that 'diverse persons' alleged they had paid him the dues for setting up their booths but could produce no warrants. The dean and assessors ordained that those who paid should receive a 'ticket' from the collector and without such a ticket it would be assumed they had not. The collector on the other hand was ordered to register the names 'in our common book as *perpetuam remanentiam*' and to produce this each year when he made up his accounts.[46] Like many other excellent rules this one seems to have been honoured more in the breach than in its observance. Even in the nineteenth century, on 10 March 1818, the collector listed about 60 non-entrants and wanted instructions as to how he should get the dues. The dean and assessors meeting had to admit that he had a difficulty here, as a former meeting supposedly deciding what fees should be had been rather vague and inaccurate, and told him to take the same sums from everyone. However, a few days later, they decided on £20 for full membership, £10 for life, £2 10s for sons and sons-in-law of members, and 10s to £1 p.a. – all sterling money now – for granting individuals a licence to carry on a trade, either wholesale or retail, but with no access to any other of the Guildry's liberties and privileges. This was to be considered at a later general meeting of the Guildry. The earlier meeting referred to as being ambiguous seems to have been held on 28 January 1807, but unfortunately the volume in which this meeting is recorded suffered quite bad fire damage.[47]

All kinds of traders were clearly defying the Guildry. One list drawn up on 13 July 1819 included a coal broker, a tobacconist, a ropemaker, a grocer, a corkcutter, a bookseller, a confectioner, a watchmaker, a wright and a slater. The people running what seems to have been a travelling zoo exhibiting wild beasts, etc. in the Fish Market were also told they must pay the Guildry 20s sterling for a licence.[48] One bookseller from Forfar, Mr. Peter Rankin, insisted that he had the right of a king's freeman to sell in Dundee but he was told to desist or risk prosecution. King's freemen were ex-servicemen and were supposed to have the freedom to trade anywhere.[49] By 1833, however, it seems as if the Guildry was prepared to compromise and perhaps accept that they could not really insist that all shopkeepers in the growing town should become members – even within the bounds of the original burgh. They agreed that non-entrants might be licensed but if payment was refused they could still be prosecuted.[50]

On one occasion when the collector had taken one offender to court for 'encroaching' on their privileges the sheriff had decreed in favour of the defender and given him his expenses, on the grounds that the Guildry should have sued him. The meeting decided to give the collector a special commission to prosecute and the clerk pointed out that his would have to be done speedily as other cases were pending.[51] On another occasion they learned that David Telfer, a cabinet maker they were pursuing, was not in fact 'encroaching' as he sold only goods of his own making in his shop, which all craftsmen were at liberty to do. Even when the abolition of the Guildry's monopoly began to appear inevitable, and was in fact supported by the incorporation, licences were being demanded in July and August 1845, although in 1844 some traders had been exempted because they were unable to pay. Licences then varied from 7s 6d to £1 1s a year, which incidentally gives us some idea of how little profit some of these shops made.[52]

After 1818, when the Guildry had gained its independence from the council, questions continued to arise about the membership. Dues had been paid to the town treasurer for both burgess ticket and guild membership and it had become the practice to enter admission to the Guildry on the burgess receipt, which was deemed illegal.[53] There was some difficulty too as to whether a would-be entrant to the Guildry for full membership for his life and posterity, who had paid the town to be a burgess only for his lifetime, qualified for the former.[54] There was also some controversy about how much should be paid by life members who wished to seek 'admission for their posterity'. From 1807, the entry fee had been raised to £20, but the magistrates had granted this for only £10 instead of the sum of £15 16s 8d actually needed to raise the fee levied for life only to £20. To avoid litigation when the Guildry became the sole controllers of entry, they allowed an extra three months to those wishing to pay the increase. In 1818 one man, Thomas Dick, was prepared to take legal action to assert his right to pay the smaller sum of £10.[55]

The procedure for entry was laid down in March 1818. First the entrant had to pay his dues to the collector, then show his stamped receipt to the council of the Guildry and produce both at the first meeting he attended.[56] Despite this the town clerk who had been paid 16s 8d to collect the Guildry's dues before 1819 seemed to have continued collecting them without being paid, as well as the money paid to the hospital fund. In 1824 the dean and assessors decided to pay him 7½% of the dues collected but the treasurer for the hospital and the kirk refused to accept dues with the deduction even of 5%. The town clerk, George Simpson, claimed he was authorised by the town council to deduct some pay and eventually it was agreed to pay him more as there were so many more citizens becoming burgesses.[57]

Despite the condition that all members should first have become burgesses, a large number of those who had paid to become guild brethren do not seem to have been very troubled by this. Nor apparently were the burghs. In the eighteenth century, in many of the royal burghs, councils apparently stopped insisting that citizens must become burgesses before being allowed to trade.[58] It does not appear that the Guildry itself was always very concerned. The numbers attending meetings had grown so much that it was not always possible to check their credentials. In September 1828, a committee appointed to prepare a correct list of guild brethren who were burgesses reported that, despite an advertisement in the local papers asking them to report with their Guildry and burgess tickets, few had paid any attention. Worse still, at the election on 1 October, when the meeting had had to adjourn to the Steeple Kirk because the guild hall was too small to accommodate the numbers attending, it emerged that some had not taken the oath before casting their votes, which legally made it null and void. Some were pensioners whose right to vote was sometimes questioned, and some were not residents, though guild brothers who had a place of business in Dundee or were partners in one were eligible. Then the position of guild brothers who were also members of the Nine and United Trades should have been checked. They had to decide whether they would vote as guild members or as craftsmen as they could not do both.[59]

However, all these questions, while they still exercised the administrators of the Guildry, began to be overshadowed as the waves of reform of various national institutions began to affect the town. Abolition of all privileges in 1846 posed a different problem by removing some of the attractions of membership, while legal obligation still remained. Pensions, stipends, salaries of officers had to be funded. The difficulty of obtaining money from the town council continued. One clerk died bankrupt and it was realised there was no point in pursuing his executors. For a time, membership did decrease, but the fact that it still had a place in Dundee's society began a revival. Men – still men only – did not join for the legal benefits that would accrue to their trade or profession; social and charitable aims were now more likely to attract them. The sons and sons-in-law of members are still granted membership on special terms.

There is one other type of member. The Guildry, like other bodies, liked to pay its respect to individuals who had served it, the town or the nation well, or who had merely won their approval for some reason or other. These were given the freedom of the Guildry, thus becoming honorary members. They showed their disapproval of George IV's treatment of his queen, by making Viscount Camperdown a free member to mark their respect for 'his manly and independent conduct' during the proceedings against her. Captain Basil Hall was honoured for his work on the question of steam boats being used on the Dundee ferries.[60] After the legal battle with the council in the second decade of the nineteenth century, Robert Rintoul, editor of the *Dundee, Perth and Cupar Advertiser* who had given so much support to the Guildry, was so honoured, as was Richard Cobden later for his part in obtaining the abolition of the Corn Laws.

NOTES

[1] DCA; G1/1, 7-10-1580.

[2] K. Brown, 'Reformation to Union,1560-1707', in R.A. Houston and W.W. Knox (eds.), *The New Penguin History of Scotland* (2001), 215.

[3] I.F. Grant, *Social and Economic Development of Scotland before 1603* (Edinburgh and London, 1930), 559.

4   D. Murray, *Early Burgh Organization in Scotland* (Glasgow, 1924), i, 488-9.

5   A. Maxwell, *The History of Old Dundee* (Edinburgh and Dundee, 1884), 46.

6   A. Maxwell, *Old Dundee, ecclesiastical, burghal and social, prior to the Reformation* (Edinburgh and Dundee,1891), 250,253.

7   DCA; G1/1, f.22. 22-9-1588.

8   DCA; G1/1, f.3.

9   DCA; G1/1, f.116.

10 DCA; G1/1, f.90. 2-2-1654.

11 A. Murray Scott, *Dundee's Literary Lives* (Dundee, 2003), i, 6.

12 F.J. Grant (ed.), *The Commissariat Record of Brechin* (S.R.S., 1902).

13 M. Lynch, 'Introduction – Scottish Towns, 1500-1700' in M. Lynch (ed.), *The Early Modern Town in Scotland* (London, 1987), 11.

14 DCA; G1/1, f.9, 12-2-1578.

15 DCA; G1/2, 30-4-1694.

16 DCA; G1/2, 10-1-1730.

17 DCA; G1/2, 29-3-1733.

18 DCA; G1/1, f.4.

19 Wyllie, 'Guildry', quote from TC minutes of 18-4-1720.

20 DCA; G1/1, 29, 10-11-1593.

21 DCA; G1/1, f.10.

22 T.M. Devine, 'The Merchant Class of the larger Scottish Towns', in G. Gordon and B.Dicks (eds.), *Scottish Urban History* (Aberdeen, 1983).

23 Smith, *United Trades, Nine Trades*, passim.

24 Maxwell, *History of Old Dundee*, 43, 44.

25 DCA; G1/2, 3-12-1722.

26 DCA; G1/2, 3-1729.

27 DCA; G1/1, ff. 85, 86; G1/2, 2-10-1730.

28 DCA; G1/1, 219.

29 DCA; G1/5, 18-2-1819.

30 DCA; G1/4, 3-1818.

31 DCA; G1/2, 9-2-1708.

32 E.C. Sanderson, 'Clothing the lieges in the Eighteenth Century', in *Archives Angus*, No.12 (June, 1996), 3-4.

33 DCA; G1/2, 3-12-1722.

34 DCA; G1/2, 6-7-1728.

35 DCA; G1/5, 30-3-1818.

36 DCA; G1/5, 23-8-1819.

37   Maxwell, *Old Dundee*, 304.

38   Warden, 196. I have to thank Mr. Dennis F. Collins for drawing my attention to this entry.

39   DCA; G1/1, f.30, 15-10-1594.

40   DCA; G1/2, 10-10-1713.

41   Warden, 161.

42   DCA; G1/5, 18-7-1825.

43   Goodfellow, 1-15, list of members

44   DCA; G1/2, 23-4-1741.

45   DCA; G1/2, 2-12-1740.

46   DCA; G1/1, f.25, 16-3-1590.

47   DCA; G1/4, March, 1818.

48   DCA; G1/5, October 1819.

49   DCA; G1/5, 22-10-1822.

50   DCA; G1/6, 18-1-1833.

51   DCA; G1/6, 24-1-1831, 2-2-1831.

52   DCA; G1/7. 6-8-1844.

53   DCA; G1/5, 30-9-1819.

54   DCA; G1/5, 12-12-1818.

55   DCA; G1/5, 29-10-1818, 14-11-1818.

56   DCA; G1/4, 19-3-1818.

57   DCA; G1/5, 7-6-1824, 5-7-1824.

58   T.M. Devine, 'The Merchant Class' in Gordon and Dick (eds.), *Scottish Urban History*, 95.

59   DCA; G1/6a, 1-9-1828, 24-9-1828, 1-10-1828.

60   Captain B. Hall R.N. *An account of the Ferry Across the Tay at Dundee 1825*, (Abertay Historical Society Reprint No.1 Dundee 1973).

3

ADMINISTRATION OF THE GUILDRY

By 1570 when *The Gildrie Book* opens it is clear that a definite administrative system was in place in the Dundee society. Meetings of members were held fairly frequently in various buildings in the town. The council-house, the tolbooth, the vestry of the town kirk, occasionally inns, are all mentioned in the minutes. Dundee Guildry did not build a hall themselves unlike many of their counterparts in Europe and England, but that was not unusual in Scotland as all the merchant guilds were so closely connected to the town councils. Stirling does have a building called the Guildhall, but it was originally built as a hospital or almshouse for poor guild brethren, burgesses and indwellers of Stirling.[1] In the eighteenth century the Guildry obtained their own premises in the elegant new town house designed by William Adam. His plans show that the council must have asked him to arrange part of the building for the use of the Guildry. There were two large rooms on the first floor, both thirty-six feet and two inches by twenty-two feet, the east one marked the 'Council House', that on the west 'The Gilderyroom'.

There seems to have been an exchange between council and Guildry in the internal arrangements of the town house between the middle of the eighteenth and the nineteenth century. In 1752, when a large quantity of peas and beans had been bought to relieve the shortage of food in the town, the shipper had been offered the use of the west room as a store.[2] It seems unlikely that the council room would have been suggested for such a purpose so presumably the west room was then the Guildry Hall. However, in 1828 a meeting adjourned to the west hall as 'the sheriff was using the guild hall'.[3] The decision to allow the additional sheriff-substitute the use of the Guild Hall and 'adjoining apartments' had apparently been made by the council 'so far as consisted with purposes for which these may be otherwise required' would seem to indicate that the east hall was by then used by the Guildry.[4] Another reference to the 'East Hall commonly called the Guild Hall' appears later in the nineteenth century but is part of the story of council/Guildry relations and it will be told in chapter 11.

General meetings of the whole body of guild brothers seem to have been held for centuries at the same time (that is 2 p.m.) until 1817. Then it was unanimously agreed to change the meeting time to 7 p.m. as the afternoon slot was 'inconvenient for many people engaged in active business'.[5] Members were for some time summoned to meetings by a bell, rung at 1.30 p.m., which hung in the tolbooth erected in 1562, until for some reason this practice was stopped and only town council meetings were called by the bell. This building needed repairs by the 1580s which were funded by some of the Guildry and in 1596 it was decided to build a new steeple of fine ashlar work on the north east corner of the tolbooth. This was an expensive and highly decorated work, with eight windows and turrets with finials on each one facing the High Street.[6] It cost almost £200, the mason's bill alone amounting to over £114.[7] Unfortunately it was rather heavy for its supporting building and when later the council added another the whole building was weakened. Partly as a result of this the tolbooth itself had to be demolished to make way for Adam's townhouse.[8] In 1819 the bell, then in the townhouse, was again tolled for general meetings of the Guildry and to summon the Dean of Guild's Court. William Clark, the jailer, applied for a gratuity for this service. He was awarded half a guinea, though, as the jail was on the top floor of the town house, he did not have far to go to carry out this duty.[9]

What can be described as the committee of management consisted of the dean, as chairman, a special group of members, given the title of assessors, and various officials, including a clerk, who acted as secretary, a collector – the treasurer – and an officer. The dean, the chief administrative officer of the Guildry, was elected by members of the association, the guild brothers, but also by the Provost of Dundee, the bailies, the town council and, according to the records, the 'whole bodie of the merchandis' of the burgh.[10] There is no indication in the earlier minutes as to whether there were rival candidates for the position of dean. On this occasion it was merely stated that Alexander Scrymgeour accepted the office and gave his oath that he would use his office 'as god sall give him grace'. The presence of the town council at the election was a legal requirement and the dean was *ex officio* a member of the council. It is possible that the council's preferred candidate was usually chosen, but for some reason, towards the end of the sixteenth century the council decided to exert more open and direct influence on the Guildry's choice.

One factor influencing the council may have been that James VI was trying to exercise more control over local councils, but perhaps it was more to do with some carelessness in the Guildry's administration. One was commented on the year after the council took over the election, and referred to a Guildry meeting held in the tolbooth in 1591, where it was stated that there had been 'long disputation and reasoning' regarding past acts and statutes which had been authenticated only by the subscription of a clerk or notary. It was decided that in future each year the dean should convene 'the haile bodie' of merchants and publicly read out all the acts made that year to be signed by them, thereby giving their consent.[11]

There may have been other areas where there was room for error or dispute, but the council's explanation for their action to a meeting of the whole council and magistrates, including the dean, and the assessors – who numbered twelve at that time – was rather different. It was claimed that confusion had arisen in the past at elections because the 'voices and suffrageis' of all the guild brothers were allowed. It was decided that the dean would in future be elected from a short leet of three councillors. These three must have held the office of bailie as well as being the 'most wyse and of greatest gravitie and best acquaint with the affairs of the gild and estaite of merchandis'. It is difficult to see how anyone could have objected to such a qualification at the time, apart from the restriction to councillors alone being eligible, and they were all guild brethren. William Duncan, a bailie the year before, was duly elected. The date and time of the election was also determined to take place at 8 a.m. or 'after prayers in the morning' in the revestry (vestry) of the kirk on the first

Monday after the election of the provost and bailies.[12] This order was repeated on several occasions, also to 'avoid confusion'. In 1576 it had been considered necessary to decree a £10 fine for the dean if he did not command his officer to give lawful warning of the time of the election while the officer was to be fined 40s for failing in this duty if he had been so commanded.[13]

Despite the attempt to avoid confusion, some arose in 1606-1607 for John Finlayson did not accept office until February 1607 though elected on 29 September 1606. However, this was the period when there was general discontent in the town over the relative positions of various groups.[14] Plague was also rampant in the town disrupting administration and society, and no doubt helping to explain that delay. These problems in the burgh could also explain why there were no more elections recorded until 1609 when the old and new councils, and the deacons of craft elected a bailie, William Goldman, as dean without any reference at all to the Guildry.[15] For the next couple of centuries the Guildry accepted this situation. The commercial interests of council and Guild were similar, the councillors were mostly merchants, apart from two craftsmen, numbering three since 1605. It was only towards the end of the eighteenth century, with the advance of reforming and democratic ideas (combined with the belief that the councillors of the time were more interested in feathering their own nests than in caring for the interests of the town) that the Guildry became restive about having no say in the choice of their dean. The result of this change in attitude manifested by the Guildry at this time will be considered in greater depth in chapters 10 and 11.

The dean was assisted by a committee of assessors: guild brothers who were expected to give him advice. In earlier days the method of choosing assessors varied from time to time, as did their numbers. In 1578 twelve were elected at the same time as the dean.[16] In 1594 twenty-four were chosen, half guild brethren, half town councillors. In 1625, the dean nominated his assessors, but 'with the consent of the provost and bailies'.[17] On 9 October, 1757 the dean announced that as this was his first court since his election he would take the opportunity of informing the meeting whom he had chosen to be assessors – beside the magistrates and the town council, which was a significant inclusion. He then named nine of whom the council had to express approval but he still seemed to have some influence in their selection. While the Dundee Guildry does not appear to have insisted on any level of wealth for their entrants as the Aberdeen society did,[18] the assessors who were active in the administration were drawn from what seems to have been a fairly small circle. But this altered over the centuries and while some Dundee names appear consistently, the surnames of deans show that the same families did not remain constantly in control.[19] In the last twenty years of the seventeenth century and the first two decades of the eighteenth, it has been shown that there was a complete change; new merchants were taking over the management.[20]

The dean and his assessors met alone increasingly as the years went by, to suggest policy which was then sometimes referred to general meetings, but often to decide on matters referred to them by such meetings. This tendency to exclude ordinary members may not have been deliberate for the attendance of all the brethren was never very certain at any meetings, despite the fines imposed on absentees. Only nine members were present at the important meeting in October 1578 at which the dean gave his accounts, and even assessors were not enthusiastic attenders, though they faced fines for absence larger than those of ordinary members. The majority of the guild brethren were in small businesses from which they could ill afford time spent on public or Guildry affairs. One dean, David Balvaird, had left office in 1714 owed £900 Scots by the Guildry, which his wife was still trying to have repaid in 1724: the reluctance to become liable for such outlay is not difficult to understand.[21]

Assessors are still important in the organisation of the Guildry. A new constitution was necessary after the town council released its hold over the incorporation and in 1818 their number was fixed at eighteen – town councillors were no longer to be eligible. The proposal that all meetings of dean and assessors should be open to all members to attend was carried on 11 October 1820, with only two dissenting votes, and in 1823 changes were again made to their election. It was approved that six should retire annually, the six at the top of the list going out of office and the newly elected six being added at the end.[22] The assessors serve for three years, and in 1869 it was decided that the six retiring were thereafter ineligible for re-election for a period of six years.

Another elected official, the collector was almost as important as the dean in the management of the society's affairs. He was elected at the same time. In 1576 he was made responsible for keeping the key of the Locked Book on the grounds that his duties included collecting all dues pertaining to the Guildry, entering these in the Book and then rendering an account of them when he retired at the end of the year before the next election. However, he could be fined £10 if he opened the book without the presence of the dean when new members were entered, after they had been examined according to 'the old acts of the society'.[23] However, Guildry regulations were altered when this was deemed necessary for the benefit of the society and the key of the Locked Book is found later to be in custody of the dean.[24] The collector also had charge of the Guildry box where their money and other valuables were kept.

One member of the administration of any organisation who is probably the most important in ensuring its efficient operation is the secretary; in the Guildry always called the clerk. It was best to have someone in the post who was legally qualified as so much of the Guildry's business was connected with legal defence of privilege. Until the nineteenth century it would seem that the town clerk usually acted as the Guildry clerk. This may help to explain the incomplete nature of the Guildry's records as the two bodies were so closely connected. His fees from the council apparently were held to cover his duties to the Guildry. However, fees were also paid to him for entering names in the Locked Book. He wrote the minutes and witnessed the members' signing their names or putting their mark beside names if they were unable to write. Most merchants were probably literate although a few are noted as simply making their mark.

While it is impossible, at least for this researcher, to find anything in the accounts to indicate regular payment to the dean and the collector, they too were apparently given some sort of financial reward at some periods. At least in the 1720s one dean offered to give up his salary when there was distress among the poor. Then at times it was proposed to give the collector a greater allowance when he had extra work, but the accounts do not give up the secret of how much. Nor do the sederunt books record any discussions on financial rewards to the dean, though any debts he had become responsible for on the Guildry's behalf would be repaid – albeit later rather than sooner as in David Balvaird's case.

The clerk gradually seems to have taken responsibility for the records as they increased in volume and more kists were required. In September 1844 the town council was asked for accommodation in the town house and provided a store room in the attics. In 1848 there was also a request for fireproofing but whether it was not carried out or was ineffective, it certainly did not prevent many of the records being scorched, water-damaged or perhaps totally lost by burning in a fire in 1911. It was interesting to find one entry in January 1870 to the effect that Mr. A.J. Warden had applied for access to the records and that the clerk was to lend him such books as he wished, 'on his obligation to return same on demand'.[25] Indeed his industry has to be admired in so far that his work, which incorporated so many of the burgh's records, was published only two years later.

Even after the Guildry won its independence from the council and appointed its own clerk, other difficulties could and did arise. In 1848 an application was made to the sheriff to enforce the delivery of books and papers from those acting for one clerk who seems to have been dismissed.[26] Some years after that, in 1864, the executor of the estate of one clerk who had died in office refused to hand over the keys to the record room and to the box in his possession without being given a receipt discharging the deceased's estate from all liability. The Guildry were very relieved to hear in February 1865 that all the papers had reached them for they included the title to a loan of £2,000 to the Harbour Trustees. When the Adam town house was demolished and replaced by the Caird Hall in the twentieth century, the records were of course moved. Today the bulk of the Guildry's archive not needed in its everyday affairs is in the care of the Dundee City archivist. Those used in its current administration are looked after by its present officers.

The other elected official in the administration was the officer, a merchant who had a variety of duties. He was a guild brother but he was also a paid official. The officer's duties must have been quite time-consuming. He had to carry messages to every member, when the dean wished to summon a meeting for instance and also execute any decrees ordered by the Guildry. In 1570 it was decided that he should be paid 4d for every person he had to contact and 2s for every decree he delivered. The society did recognise what was involved for the merchant concerned; he had to run round Dundee, small as the original royalty was, to contact members and he was provided with shoes and as late as 1852 with a new gown at a cost of £2 15s.[27] One of his duties was attendance at funerals of members. In 1830 he was given a new hat and gown specially for these solemn occasions.

One important support for him when he was carrying out some of his duties was that he was allowed to enrol eight to ten members to assist him to deliver decrees; any who refused were fined 8s. Further, he was also given power to 'poynd and distress' (take the goods) of any member who was withholding dues or fines pertaining to the Guildry, without involving any officer of law. On such occasions 'no crime was to be imputed to him'. In other words he was given immunity from any possible legal process arising from such seizures.[28] The officer was appointed at the same time as the dean. Olipher Lindsay, who had been Alexander Scrymgeour's officer in 1570, was re-elected in 1576 and must have given satisfaction as he was still occupying the position in October 1584. The officer's involvement in the financial business of the Guildry, in for instance collecting fines, could give rise to problems. When one officer, James Watson, died it emerged that there were some inconsistencies in his accounts. His widow eventually admitted to the treasurer that she had used part of the incorporation's funds to take out insurance on her husband's life. It took the threat of legal proceedings to persuade her to repay the money.[29]

The duties of all these members of the administration were important for the well-being of the society but the dean's responsibilities were the heaviest. His first duty in the eyes of his fellow members was to the Guildry to ensure that they lost none of the privileges of being a free merchant burgess in a royal burgh. To maintain these privileges the Guildry were prepared to put their hands in their pockets. Five days after Alexander Scrymgeour was elected in 1570, for example, the 'whole bodie of merchants and the brethren of gild' unanimously agreed to make a contribution to him and any eight assessors to help them pursue 'diligent remeid' if anything occurred to damage existing privileges or any 'novations' which might seem to threaten them. Any who refused such assistance would be fined £5 to be put in the Guildry box where all their funds, documents and artefacts (called their evidents) were kept. The size of the fine shows how important they considered this aspect of the Guildry's management to be.

All merchants, whether guild brethren or not, were burgesses and wished to continue to enjoy the monopoly of trade which was legally that of the royal burghs. To carry out such duties the dean had to be sure of their support. A few days after Scrymgeour's election the merchants promised 'by their hands upholden to fortify, maintain and give obedience' to the dean in the 'doing of his office'. They also promised not to speak 'irreverently or injuriously' or to the dean's 'defamation'.[30] The need to accept his authority and show due respect to the office was recognised throughout the Guildry's history even when the man was elected by the council. In 1618 a merchant, A. Miln, had asserted that the dean was 'partial' in a case where he was the defendant and for that he was fined £10 for 'misbehaving' himself to the dean and was imprisoned until he asked the dean's pardon.[31]

While the collector may initially have been in charge of the Guildry's box, it is plain that the dean had fairly free access to funds as he had often to lay out money on behalf of the society. Each year he, like the collector, had to 'make his compt' three or four days before the election of his successor or his own re-election. In 1727, one merchant, James Ramsay, protested against the dean using the Guildry's money without the consent of the assessors and prepared to take legal action on this. As he was an assessor there is probably more to this than appears in the minutes. However, the provost and the dean answered that his protestation seemed to be more calculated for 'making disturbance and division than for any good of gildrie' and made it plain that the dean had discretionary powers to act in the Guildry's interest. No more was heard of this.[32]

On the actual day of the election the dean also had to hand over to his successor all the 'evidents' which had been in his care during his time in office. The incoming dean accepted the locked kist or box and signed for these. Unfortunately, despite this annual inspection the contents did vary quite dramatically over the years. It was decided in 1606 to have an inventory drawn up by seven elected members on the grounds that 'for 200 years bygone the said evidents had been confusedly received and delivered but (i.e. without) inventory' which had 'hurt the estate of gildrie'.[33] By this time the kist had three locks, the dean keeping the principal key, the oldest bailie, and the collector the other two. Six years later there were two boxes with a list of some of the contents: the joug, the pint jug for measuring liquids; the elwand, the cloth measure; the key for the kist in which the stone weights were kept; the burning iron for marking firlots, one of the grain measures. Mortcloths were not mentioned at this point but they appeared in later inventories with their 'pocks' – the pokes or bags in which they were kept when not in use. In 1695 it was the retiring collector who handed over the weights and the mortcloth, but in 1825 the officer had been looking after the weights and measures.[34]

The dean's position brought prestige but his responsibilities were really very heavy both within the Guildry and in public affairs. Attendance at head courts, at council meetings, and officiating at the freighting of ships, though a bailie could act alone there; signing every charterparty and sometimes having to keep the document; serving on practically every committee that the Guildry set up on any matter, apart from chairing every meeting with his assessors and every general meeting, at which he had to maintain discipline; riding the marches and informing assessors that he expected them to accompany him; and calling a meeting of Dundee taxpayers when a new tax was to be imposed to hear their views. All these duties must have taken toll of the dean's time. Dundee deans may have been thankful that by the time we have any of their records they were at least not expected to find husbands for their fellow guild members' daughters or, failing that, to place them in religious houses.[35] In theory every guild brother could aspire to such office but obviously thriving businesses with good staff were essential to working deans, and possibly family wealth besides.

Another aspect of the Guildry's administrative machinery in which the dean had judicial powers was the Dean of Guild Court, at which he was originally accompanied by assessors and which met every Tuesday at 2 p.m. Absent assessors were fined 5s in the sixteenth century, 6s at the beginning of the seventeenth and 12s by 1671. Records of the court are to be found mixed up with those of the town's head court and with the Guildry's own minutes. One volume in the Guildry records which has been rebound and is largely illegible in parts is described as the Minutes of the Guild Court, but it is often only when the minutes include the words 'this court' that it is possible to know whether it is a judicial assembly or merely a business meeting of the dean and assessors.[36] The court dealt with breaches of Guildry ordinances and with all disputes between merchants, who were fined £5 if they went to other judges before laying their cases before the dean.

In 1588 rules and regulations deciding the behaviour of all who attended were laid down.[37] The officer was given his instructions and it was his duty to warn the defender in any action between merchants that he must bring such witnesses and proof as the pursuer demands, and that non-appearance by anyone connected in a case would mean fines. During sessions of the court there was to be no 'conference', private or public, from the time the dean sat down until he rose, and 'reverence' was to be shown not only to the dean but to each other's neighbours. These rules were designed to make sure that cases could be properly heard, as well as the opinions of the merchants most able to assist the dean.

Cases included disputes of all sorts between merchants at home and abroad. Three skippers were fined in 1617 for not presenting charterparties to the dean to be underwritten by him. On the same day William Jack was fined £3 and kept in ward for insulting William

Ramsay.[38] Alex Rankin had neither had the dean present when he freighted his ship, the *Read Lyon*, nor had he registered it on his return.[39] In another case a dispute was heard 'on behalf of bairns' in 1624. Their father's partner was accused of cheating them out of their share of a deal in wine and tar.[40] In 1754 the collector, Andrew White, had obtained a sentence before the magistrates against a hammerman, Thomas Scott, who had encroached on the privileges of the Guildry when he was not a member. Scott had appealed to the Lords of Justiciary to be heard at their next circuit and the collector wanted advice from the court as to whether he should discuss it before the Lords. The answer was positive.[41] The Guildry was not going to lose a case by default.

There are innumerable cases throughout the records of which those mentioned above are only a small part. From the rules laid down in 1588 it would appear that for some time anyone who was a Guildry member could attend the court. In 1595, however, just as the council had commented on the confusion of having too many voting, the dean's court also became distinctly elitist. The comment was made that 'great disorder and confusion' resulted from seeking the opinions of every member on civil cases, which were of course its main business. A great number of those adding to the debate were described as 'not well skilled in matters of importance'. In future only the dean and his assessors were to vote and the 'whole multitude' were to be excluded.[42] In 1712 a quorum of fifteen was decreed for any guild court and was to be used for determining any matter belonging to the Guildry. Anything to which all members agreed, however, would be considered a valid subject for discussion.[43]

One unique and important meeting of the court was held in September 1726, attended by 'a great many more merchants, shipmasters and guild brethren of this burgh and others'. The business to be discussed would affect the economy of all Scotland. The Convention of Royal Burghs, which was to meet in November, had requested that the burghs should give their views before that meeting as to how the money coming into Scotland as a result of the Treaty of Union should be spent.[44] The Board of Trustees for Improving Fisheries and Manufactures was established in 1727 by this great infusion of cash into the Scottish economy.

In the middle of the seventeenth century the court had begun to look at questions regarding property. New building, renovations and alterations had to be sanctioned by the Dean of Guild Court, where the effect on adjacent properties and on public highways was always taken into account. For instance, an oven which could be a risk to neighbours' property had to have strong walls round it, while at the same time being careful not to obstruct neighbours' lights through their windows.[45] The dean could order the demolition of ruinous houses if there was danger from falling slates, etc. and on one occasion decreed that the material removed was to be rouped to cover the costs.[46] One man had reason for complaint against his neighbour's neglect of his property. John Maxwell's wife's school, presumably a dame's school held in his house, was losing pupils as parents withdrew them for fear of the children being hurt by slates falling off Alexander Duncan's house on their way to school. Duncan's house was inspected and the dean appointed slaters to take off loose slates.[47] The records of the decisions of the courts illustrate a great deal of the history of the town's buildings and as one can see, some social history.

Gradually many of the cases which might have been heard by the dean became subsumed into the magistrates' jurisdiction but the control over property remained with the Dean of Guild Court. It may have suited town councils to have such matters dealt with in such a way, even though the Court of Session declared the dean's jurisdiction to be different from those of the provost and bailies.[48] The records of the court were damaged badly in the 1911 fire and as a result there is a gap in information about its proceedings between the later eighteenth and the nineteenth century. After becoming independent of the council various questions arose about the court's management as well as about the general administration of the incorporation, but as a result the court gained a new lease of life. A member of the Guildry, David Blair, junior, who was dean in 1819, and who had been active in the various quarrels with the council hitherto, prepared a new set of rules, but even so there were several disagreements, especially about the position of the procurator fiscal.[49]

Other towns with Merchant Guilds had been applied to for some guidance but it was noted that all the rules had been 'digested' from those of the Glasgow court.[50] In addition, Mr. James Ivory, the Edinburgh advocate, was employed to give his opinion and to give it speedily as the court could not do its work without certainty about its judicial position. Ivory asked for the use of 'the ancient records' before he would begin.[51]

The court once constituted as a court separate from the council had to appoint its own officials. Previously the town clerk had acted as clerk and legal adviser but in 1819 James Saunders became clerk and legal assessor. The same person occupied both these posts until 1838 when the dean and his assessors decided to recommend to the general meeting in the following October that the two should be separated.[52] A totally new post had to be filled, that of procurator fiscal to the court whose duties would have previously been carried out by a bailie and Thomas Smart, senior, was appointed. The dean thought he should appoint the fiscal and some members of the Guildry felt that this should be the responsibility of the whole incorporation. One meeting decided that that official did not need a salary as all he had to do was to present 'blank processes of a public nature' for which he got ordinary dues.[53] However, in 1828 Smart was granted ten guineas per year for the unpaid trouble he had taken.

The Dean of Guild's Court retained control over new erections, alterations and demolitions in the ancient royalty of Dundee, subject to appeals to higher courts, until local government in Scotland was reorganised in 1975, though there was a slightly doubtful period between 1831 and 1833. The town had been disenfranchised over disagreements about the election of dean in 1827 and the new set in 1831 made no provision for the Guildry to elect a dean. The procurator fiscal, still Thomas Smart, ignored this but in 1833 the act which reformed burgh government[54] restored to the Dundee Guildry its right to elect its own dean and his jurisdiction, with a place on the town council, as it did in Edinburgh, Glasgow, Aberdeen and Perth. In all other burghs in which a Guildry existed the office and title were to cease.

The jurisdiction of the dean was not universally popular. It was always subject to appeal to superior courts and there was a vitriolic attack on it in 1825 referring to the possibility of appeals to the Court of Session. The lower court was described as the 'most perfect snare for litigation human ingenuity could have contrived' and that mutual walls were an inexhaustible source of litigation. The writer also claimed that in burghs 'not encumbered with this legal machine' there were no such disputes - which one may take leave to doubt.[55] A draft bill on burgh reform had suggested abolition, and two commissions on the law courts – one in 1834 and another in 1869 – also recommended this. Support from local M.P.s however saved Dundee's Dean of Guild Court as well as those previously mentioned above. Views changed, however, and the Burgh Police (Scotland) Act of 1892 not only confirmed the existing jurisdiction of the Dean of Guild Courts but gave power to set up new ones, while in 1947 any burgh without one was ordered to establish one, consisting of the dean and several councillors.[56]

The powers of the court in Dundee over buildings were never extended beyond the old royalty of the old burgh and in 1820 it was decided to have a map made showing its boundaries clearly; also the various districts which the Guildry had delineated were to be painted in different colours and numbered.[57] Considering how the town had expanded, this was a wise move. Though the royalty was a small area, within its limits the Dean of Guild's powers were considerable where property was concerned. From 1871 the Dundee Police and Improvement Act vested control over buildings in the rest of the city in the Works Committee of the Police Commissioners (later in the town council). Owners in the old royalty had to have permission from both the Dean of Guild court and the Works Committee before they could build, alter or extend their property.[58] There seems to have been only one instance where the dean's court's authority was challenged absolutely, in a case against David Stewart in 1828.[59]

This long-lasting Scottish legal institution was abolished by the 1973 Local Government (Scotland) Act which passed on the ancient jurisdiction of Dean of Guild Court to 'the authority responsible for building control in the area concerned', just as it abolished town councils. The dean in Dundee, called Lord Dean after 1889, then lost his unusual position as an *ex officio* member of Dundee town council. In at least two periods the dean held the casting vote over the elected members when the political parties in the council were equally divided – a situation which cannot have pleased the elected members.[60]

NOTES

[1]   Morris, *The Stirling Merchant Gild*, 301.
[2]   DCA; G1/2, 14-3-1752.
[3]   DCA; G1/6a, 2-10-1828.
[4]   *Report on Municipal Corporations* (London, 1835), 237.
[5]   DCA; G1/4b, 19-4-1817.
[6]   DCA; G1/1, f.75.
[7]   DCA; G1/1, f.75
[8]   Maxwell, *History of Old Dundee*, 149-50.
[9]   DCA; G1/5, 24-6-1819, 18-11-1819.
[10]   DCA; G1/1, f.5, 13-10-1570.
[11]   DCA; G1/1, ff. 25, 26, 6-5-1591, 23-9-1591.
[12]   DCA; G1/1, f.24, 29-9-1590.
[13]   DCA; G1/1, f.7, 10-10-1576.
[14]   See Chapter 8, The Guildry's Relations with the Dundee Trades.
[15]   DCA; G1/1, f.38.
[16]   DCA; G1/1, f.10, 16-10-1578.
[17]   DCA; G1/1, f.51, 4-10-1625.
[18]   Devine, 'Merchant Class', 100.
[19]   Warden, 222-24.
[20]   Devine, 'Merchant class', 101-102.
[21]   DCA; G1/2, 18-1-1724, 7-3-1724.
[22]   DCA; G1/5, 29-9-1823.
[23]   DCA; G/1, f.8.
[24]   DCA; G1/1, f.49, 1619.
[25]   DCA; G1/8, 27-1-1870.

[26] DCA; G1/7, 31-5-1848.

[27] DCA; G1/7, 13-6-1852.

[28] DCA; G1/1, f.6, 2-11-1570.

[29] DCA; G1/7, 26-4-1843, 28-11-1843.

[30] DCA; G1/1,f.6, 2-11-1570.

[31] Warden, 151.

[32] DCA; G1/2, 8-11-1727.

[33] DCA; G1/1, f.38, 10-2-1606.

[34] DCA; G1/1, 4-10-1695, G1/5, 20-12-1825.

[35] DCL; Lamb 195 (22).

[36] DCA; G1/2.

[37] DCA; G1/1, f.22, 29-9-1588.

[38] DCA; G1/1, f.47, 28-1-1617.

[39] DCA; G1/1, f.48, 8-4-1617.

[40] DCA; G1/1, f.54.

[41] DCA; TC56/2, 30-3-1754.

[42] DCA; G1/1, f.32, 20-9-1595.

[43] DCA; G1/2,2a, 26-1-1712.

[44] DCA; G1/2, 5-9-1726.

[45] DCA; G1/2, 3-10-1733.

[46] DCA; G1/2, 2-7-1707.

[47] DCA; G1/2, 13-11-1724.

[48] A. M. Jackson, *Glasgow Dean of Guild Court: a history* (Glasgow, 1983), 47.

[49] The rules are to be found complete in Warden, 209-221.

[50] DCA; G4/1, 10-11-1819.

[51] DCA; G1/5, November 1819.

[52] DCA; G1/6, 12-1-1838.

[53] DCA; G1/5, 5 and 10-10-1821.

[54] 3 & 4 William IV, c. 76.

[55] DCL; Lamb 195 (23).

[56] Jackson, *Glasgow Dean of Guild Court*, 116.

[57] DCA; G1/5, 6-1-1820.

[58] I. Gray, *A Guide to Dean of Guild Court Records* (Glasgow, 1994), 34.

[59] DCA, Gavin Cowper, Typescript of his description of the Dean of Guild Court records, 1814-1818 (1999), 7.

[60] Information from Mr. David Goodfellow and Mr. Dennis F. Collins.

4

ENJOYMENT AND DEFENCE
OF PRIVILEGE

Scottish merchants had benefited from legislation and royal favour throughout the centuries. The Scottish government was not alone, of course, in giving favourable treatment to specific towns, the royal burghs, and their inhabitants, when their trading activities could be of benefit to the monarch and the economy of the country. Cities in Europe can be found acting in similar ways. In Lille, for instance, the son of a citizen would pay a sum that can be translated as 4s 2d to inherit his father's status while another without such a connection would be faced with a fee of 60s.[1] The Guildry was well aware of how important it was to be exactly sure of their rights and one of Alexander Scrymgeour's earliest moves after his election on 23 October 1570 was to appoint a group of eight members to convene and collect all the 'liberties of merchants' and to make a list of all relevant acts and statutes for the benefit of future deans. The short list on the title page of *The Gildrie Book* may be the preliminary result of this collection but it is a scanty survey compared to what appeared later in the book covering both sides of ff.12-17. This later collection was described at its beginning as the result of an order of 1580.[2] What dean Scrymgeour ordered was of course a major task and it is likely that the clerk of the Guildry, usually a lawyer, was probably the person most responsible for its compilation. It is unlikely that even merchants, as cultured as we know some of them were,[3] would have had the necessary knowledge of law or the ability or even the time to find and read all the necessary sources.

The first acts listed were 'drawn furth of the buk of the law called *Regiam Majestatem*', a collection of medieval Scots law, and are undated except by chapter number. They are followed by these taken from 'the buk of the actis of parliament' with the name of the monarch reigning at the time in the margin: from James I to James VI. Next come those passed in Dundee itself and finally those out of the 'Sea Laws'. This last entry would seem to date the Guildry's recording of the collection of the laws much later than 1580 as *The Sea Law of Scotland* by William Welwood was published in 1590.[4] Such a delay is not to be wondered at considering how much work would be involved in obtaining this comprehensive survey of merchants' privileges and duties. They are worth examining as they certainly do provide the officers of the Guildry with the necessary legal knowledge with which they could both protect their members from encroachments on their legal rights and prevent or punish breaches of any of the restrictions on their trading methods by members or anyone else.

The first extract from *Regiam Majestatem* lays down 'of him that is made burgess' that he must first swear fealty to the king and to the bailies of the town where he became burgess. All these earlier laws refer to burgesses not to merchant guilds, but burgesses alone could become merchants or craft masters, so that in effect any guild was bound by them. Medieval trade was hemmed round with restrictions and the business activities of burgesses who, despite their description as freemen, were not immune from these bonds. The burgess could use his freedom only in the burgh where he obtained it, and within the burgh he could trade only with other free burgesses except during fairs, when stallangers, small traders, could come into town with their goods. Not only could burgesses not trade with unfree, they were not allowed to act as factors for them unless permitted by the dean. Forestalling and regrating, that is buying up goods before they could reach the market and buying in bulk to hoard and sell, were strictly forbidden to all, as both of these practices gave the buyer an unfair advantage in medieval eyes. Craftsmen could sell only goods of their own or their servants' making. Foreign merchants could deal only with burgesses even if they did not mean to export goods. Burgesses were allowed to keep weights and measures in their own houses, but these had to be marked with the burgh's seal to ensure their accuracy.

The import/export trade was also carefully regulated. The first concern of government seemed to be that anyone trading abroad should have resources ample enough to bear the great risk that might be incurred in dangerous voyages across the seas. Without a certain amount of wealth in goods, either his own or 'committed to his governance', a merchant was not eligible to ship goods out of the country. In the reigns of James I and James II that amount was defined as a serplath of wool, i.e. three large bags, or half the last, the cargo, of the ship.[5] Freighting was carefully monitored too. A charterparty, the written contract referring to the hiring of a ship or part of it, was deemed essential and later the Guildry decided that it should be kept by the dean, after he had seen it signed by the two parties involved, the master and the merchant. It was usual at one period to tear it in two with each of the contractors keeping half. The need for the dean's presence at the loading was removed in the Decreet Arbitral but by the time the *Gildrie Book* was opened the Guildry had apparently resumed this duty.[6] A bailie would also be in attendance and sometimes acted alone.

Another privilege that accrued to the Guildry was that goods brought into the burgh for sale, whether by sea or land, by any who were not burgesses of the town should first be offered to the society. This rule did not of course apply to cargoes which belonged to local merchants. When the Guildry definitely refused goods offered, then the seller was at liberty to find a private buyer (though under certain conditions). In 1693 the local collector of customs, Alexander Swintoune, offered 1800 deal 'or thereabout' at £52 10s which the Guildry court refused. He was allowed to sell the wood but not cheaper than the price offered to the Guildry.[7] Another offer the Guildry refused was made by David Simson, a lawyer in Anstruther, who had apparently been doing some dealing on his own. He wanted to bring in goods from Danzig – free of custom duty – consisting of lint, ropes, fine iron and five and a half 'chock of knapoll, five feet long'. A chock was a set of 60 pieces and 'knapoll' was board used as barrel staves or panelling. He was allowed to sell these to freemen only on payment of £100 Scots to the Guildry.[8]

On the other hand, if Guildry and seller could not agree about a price the importer could be in difficulties. In 1706 one dealer, Mitchell Leg from Stavanger, offered a cargo of timber cut to various sizes at

12 dollars per hundred. The Guildry offered 10 dollars for the largest pieces (8, 9 and 10 feet long and 8, 9 and 10 inches broad) and less for various other cuts. This was refused and the skipper was forbidden to sell his cargo within the burgh. Not surprisingly he compromised and the guild brethren divided the cargo among themselves, 'according to the stent' - the amount they paid in taxes.[9] The town council also had some claim to be offered goods coming into the port. In 1642 William Parker was fined for buying some 'oylie' (oil) from Norway which had not been offered to the council and Patrick Nicol, the Arbroath man who had sold it to him, was also fined.[10] The apparently conflicting claims of Guildry and council do not seem to have caused any problems between the two bodies, despite or perhaps because of the fact that the Guildry was in effect a branch of the council responsible for trade and commerce. And of course at that time the council elected the dean.

In theory the royal burghs and their merchant burgesses held monopolistic powers over trade and commerce, but there were regular infringements of the rules, not only by the unfree inhabitants of the burghs and strangers or foreigners. Throughout the records of Dundee head court, which also includes meetings of the Dean of Guild Court, there are very many cases, rather more than can be described in this volume, where offenders against the trading regulations are tried and usually found guilty. Forestalling and regrating, though forbidden, were commonly practised in all burghs and town councils had to be vigilant in maintaining trading rules considered vital to the town's prosperity. Dundee town council records show how the council reacted and how even burgesses and members of the Guildry of Dundee and of other burghs ignored the rules if they could make a profit. In 1638 a Stirling baker was discovered to have been buying in bulk from the public market and was threatened with a fine of £150 if he was found guilty of this again. Thomas Nicoll, the Dundee mealmaker, who had been the seller, was fined only £5.[11] The Convention of Royal Burghs also tried to enforce all the trading rules, with limited success. In 1615 meeting at St. Andrews the commissioners had to order Dunfermline and Culross to stop indwellers from Torryburn, not a royal burgh, from 'using the trad of merchandise', thereby usurping the liberties of free burghs.[12] In 1620 Crail and Kirkcudbright were asked to restrain such actions too.

Maintaining the Guildry privileges was a never-ending struggle. Officers had to be continually on the watch for offenders against the national and burgh legislation as well as its own rules which were binding on members. Offenders often came from their own ranks, and it is unlikely that unfree Dundonians or strangers coming into the town, who did not share in official Guildry or merchant privilege, would have been successful in their dealings if many local guild brethren and other free burgesses had not connived at their activities. In 1591 the Guildry had to deal with a complaint 'by certain of neighbours upon ane great disorder lately fallen within ye burgh' through secret pacts and agreements about prices of 'unfreemens warris' before they were offered to the town. This was described as 'great prejudice to the guild brethren'. It was decided that anyone found attempting to make such arrangements with unfree traders about goods arriving in the port by sea from home ports or abroad would be fined £10 Scots for every £100 worth of goods he bought, quite a hefty amount.[13] Another offence was committed by Robert Watson who was summoned in December 1603 to answer the charge that he had acted for foreigners in selling wine from Bordeaux without offering it first to the town.[14]

The brewers complained in 1712 that a bailie of the town, a magistrate who should have been ensuring that the rules were obeyed, was buying up coal from importers and selling at high prices to the town, despite town and Guildry regulations.[15] Another bailie was accused of selling goods belonging to a Montrose man to a Dundee merchant; this deal was for a hogshead of jumps – strips of leather used to build up the heels of shoes.[16] The prominent merchant and landowner, George Dempster, was reported by the collector, Charles Jobson, to have bought about 53 bolls of north country meal, meant for the market. On this occasion the court decided to wait until the next meeting to make any decisions on this and no more seems to have been heard of it.[17] Some merchants got round the rules by sending their wives to deal and then denying all knowledge of such activities, while one woman, a Mrs. Murray, who must have been trading in cloth, sent her servants to neighbouring merchants' shops to buy goods for her. This caused the Guildry some concern as they were not sure if there were any acts of the Guildry court against such practices.[18]

Some cases regarding wool particularly illuminate how widespread breaches of the rules were and how easy it was to circumvent them, if both buyers and sellers were so inclined. Statutes had been made over the centuries forbidding private wool sales and all dealing was supposed to take place in the open market. Yet in 1613, two St. Andrews merchants, John Vennison and John Anderson confessed that for twelve years they had been selling great quantities of wool, each of five or six stone, to neighbours as well as inhabitants of Dundee and 'uthers resorting thereto' in private booths, lofts and houses in Dundee. They were fined £3 plus the value of the wool which should have been confiscated but was presumably untraceable and this comparatively light fine was explained because they had confessed to their crimes.[19] Despite this, three years later, merchants of St Andrews, Perth and Cupar were each fined £5 for the same offence,[20] and later still more merchants from St. Andrews and Cupar had to agree not to sell or buy wool except on the 'high market gait' during public markets.[21]

There were occasional amendments or qualifications to the rules, when it suited the organisation. For instance in 1711, when there was need to obtain more money to cover a specific debt, it was decided that guild members could buy from strangers - paying 1% of the value of the goods to the Guildry if the other trader had been approved by the society, and 2% if he had not.[22]

Guild brethren were expected to use local vessels and their local harbour, and to carry each others' goods. Another way of avoiding taxes and fees resulting from this had been discovered by the early seventeenth century, or at least it emerged in the Guildry records then. Indeed, it may have been going on for quite a while longer. By 1609, many local merchants had begun to freight ships of all sizes – ships, crears, boats – from the inhabitants of the South Ferry and other strangers, who were of course not Dundee burgesses. They were also carrying the goods of these traders in preference to those of their fellow inhabitants. By so doing they avoided the payments due to a royal burgh and the need to deal with the dean. A fine of £100 was to be imposed on any who offended in this way when goods of Dundonians could be just as easily be obtained. The somewhat obscure accounts of the society do not show signs of massive fines accruing to the funds. The need to consult the dean in future before ships from the South Ferry were freighted was ratified and it may be that traders covered themselves by approaching the dean.[23]

One group of traders was always a problem as they were neither residents nor burgesses and persistently broke Guildry rules. These were chapmen and hawkers, travelling traders, who were supposed to have permission from the Guildry before they could sell their goods in the town except on market days, and they were certainly not expected to open shops without that permission. One traveller was fined for opening a booth without permission in 1601.[24] The hawkers carried their goods on their backs or in baskets and wandered round from town to town. The chapmen tended to be more ambitious and daring; in 1607 three had their goods confiscated by the collector. They had set up stands on the 'calsay' (the causeway) to sell foreign wares, when only goods made in this country were permitted to such dealers.[25] Possibly most came into the towns only on market days and sold more to country customers, but in the eighteenth century they began to seem more of a threat. For some reason those selling cutlery as well as other 'toys' seemed to be most worrying, and in 1734 the Dean of Guild Court was adamant that they could sell only on market days and in the market place.[26] This may not have totally satisfied the shopkeepers and merchants for in 1738, after a complaint, they were asked to give a list of names and of particular grievances,[27] but nothing seems to have resulted from this, and as we have seen, there were also problems then about the number of small shops being opened in the town.

In 1822 another attempt began to control hawkers. One guild brother requested action against them as they did not pay taxes or join the Guildry and this gave them financial advantage over shopkeepers. Other guilds in Perth, Aberdeen, Arbroath, Montrose and Cupar were consulted and it emerged that there was no unity of method of dealing with hawkers. In Cupar they were allowed to go from door to door which the Dundee Guildry simply wrote off as erroneous practice.[28] Aberdeen had no hawkers as they were aware the dean of guild there would resist their presence; all attempts to operate in that town after the passing of a recent Hawkers and Pedlars Act had been promptly checked. The Aberdeen authorities thought the new act did not confer new privileges. Montrose thought the new act did not supersede guildry rules and one hawker, Isaac Leven, who had tried legal action, had given up. Arbroath thought the same while Perth had pedlars only on market day and in the market place.

Dundee for forty years had taken the same dues from strangers and hawkers for the liberty of selling for a temporary period, but the Guildry considered that this was an example of the magistrates neglecting their duties while they were managing Guildry affairs. Stronger action was thought necessary and handbills were to be printed to let it be known to hawkers that they could sell only on market days and at the market place, unless they had purchased their freedom from the Guildry.[29] This was not the end of the matter. In 1825 some members of the Guildry expressed the wish to consult counsel regarding their privileges, including where they stood on the subject of hawkers, as the magistrates still refused to act against those men who, it was claimed, sold inferior goods then left the town without bothering to defend themselves. The legal reply was not encouraging - the Dean of Guild Court was not one which could deal with this.[30] However, some hawkers took evasive action by consigning their goods to an auctioneer or a shopkeeper to avoid payment of Guildry dues. In 1819 the clerk had been ordered to prosecute David Farquharson who helped a hawker in this way, and another who 'under his cloak' was selling books and stationery at a Castle Street shop.[31]

It is probable that many more merchants and traders broke the Guildry's rules and encroached on their privileges than were ever prosecuted before the Dean of Guild's Court. If legal action was taken against any offenders, however, that court's jurisdiction was rarely questioned. The legal powers of the royal burghs and of the Guildry, where such existed, were generally accepted, even before the rediscovery of the Merchants' Letter in Dundee. They could also be supported in all the courts of the country: until, that is, parliament passed the legislation which removed the special position of all royal burghs and the incorporations within them in 1846. The various cases noted here help to illustrate how the system worked and how widespread were the effects of these privileges on traders and trading.

Defending all their privileges, sometimes by recourse to the law-courts, meant that the Guildry needed a reasonable income. For example, taking a protest to the head court cost money, including apparently fees to the dean and the officer for performing their duties there.[32] Merchants had to pay one fee to join and another for 'upsetting their booths' which were usually simply stalls set up outside their houses. They also paid the officer and the clerk for entering their names in the Locked Book. Fees varied throughout the centuries, usually increasing; in 1645-46 Alex Johnston had to pay £40 Scots for his booth.[33] After the Reformation, the changes in religious observance ensured that the taxes on goods designated in the Merchants' Letter for the upkeep of the Halie Bluid Altar would not be used for that purpose. As the earlier records are missing it is not possible to say when these moneys were transformed into the 'gild silver' and used for general purposes. The fees or fines including wine and wax, for the candles and wine used by the priest, gradually disappeared. Then one collector, Walter Hay, had noted that he had not been able to collect all the money due for the years 1580-1583 with the result that his returns were short by £102 7s 2d. By 1588 to avoid such losses, it was decided to roup the gild silver, with the glass timer running for half an hour, during which period all bids had to be made. The highest bidder paid what he had offered to the collector, and whether he lost or gained by the transaction the Guildry at least knew how their funds stood.[34] The sums varied each year, with Walter Hay bidding £38 in 1591 despite his losses in previous years,[35] while in 1612, £48 was bid.[36]

Despite the benefits of the system of employing a tacksman to collect the funds, it would appear that this was not wholly successful. In 1592 a meeting in the tolbooth attended by the town council was convened to consider complaints made regarding the 'oversight' of the Guildry tacksmen. It emerged that they were taxing only staple goods that were being exported. Too many goods thereby escaped taxation and this was 'to the great hurt and prejudice' of the whole estate as well as the Guildry. In future it was declared customs must be paid both 'without and within this realm' and new dues were decided on for goods at home and abroad, with some foreign prices being fixed in foreign currency.[37] As Walter Hay had not managed to collect all the money due the decade before, and yet had become tacksman in 1591, he may have been responsible for the most recent deficiencies in the customs collection. However, the rouping continued until the civil wars disrupted this arrangement like so many other aspects of Dundee life. As the Guildry had never formally stopped the rouping, it was decided in 1680 to ask the town council's agreement that it should be revived, but this does not seem to have happened.

Another source of income came from renting mortcloths, usually velvet with silk fringes, for covering coffins before burial. Most societies kept these for their members. They were of varying sizes, large for adults and small for children, and were a considerable source of income – £67 16s Scots in 1697.[38] Mortcloths were not cheap to buy or to keep in good repair but members and their families must have appreciated being able to hire them when deaths occurred. Members were expected to attend funerals of their fellow guild brethren and these were ceremonious occasions: the funeral procession led by a mute and the coffin attended by sallies, whose gloves, caps – in 1830 made out of the old mortcloths! – stockings and shoes were paid for by the Guildry. The accounts for 1797-98 include 8s 6d for six pairs of black gloves, 17s 6d for hose and 4s for buckles. However in 1824 the Guildry found that they could not insist that their members used the incorporation's mortcloths, nor could they compel them to pay when another society's cloth had been used.[39] At that point it was decided to keep them in good repair but by 1854 it appeared that their charges were so much higher – 5s compared to 1s 8d for the Wrights for the largest size – that use of the incorporation's mortcloths was decreasing. Charges were lowered then, but in 1869 two guild brethren were appointed to sell the Guildry's stock.[40]

Despite their expenses the Guildry seem to have been able to save and invested their surplus finds in various ways. In November 1598, they decided that they would have their 'haill silver', all their funds, lent out to 'private persons' returned to them before Whitsunday

1599. They had decided it would be more safely bestowed upon 'sure heritable and irredeemable rent' which would remain with the 'estate of gildrie' of Dundee for ever. Then it could be applied to the particular uses 'contained in erection of said gildrie and special actis maid by deans of the time'.[41] In other words they meant to buy property. What they may have bought at that time is not certain, but over the years they had houses all over the old town, including several in the Nethergate, in Tendalls Wynd, Couttie's Wynd and also they seemed to have an interest in the Castle Mills. The 1706-7 accounts show £841 13s Scots being paid to the town council for three acres of land on the east side of the Hilltown, which they decided to wadset rather than feu, which meant that the land could be redeemed. In addition the town council borrowed from them and later they deposited money with the Harbour Board. These all brought in annual interest, which can be seen in their accounts.[42] Profit from the property was rather variable, for ground annuals and rents are more often shown as being in arrears than fully paid. In the 1650-51 accounts, another of the hazards of letting property appeared, when £13 6s 8d had to be spent on tenements that were 'not habitable'. It is also unclear in the records in Dundee City Archive whether houses were sold or not, but in 1848, after the death of one clerk, when only legal action had persuaded his executors to return the Guildry's papers, it was discovered that the title deeds to their property were missing and the new clerk had been unable to trace them.

In May 1696, like so many other Scots and Scottish institutions, the Guildry made an investment which lost them quite a lot of money. The dean and twelve assessors decided to use £200 sterling of their stock to buy shares in the Company of Scotland trading to Africa and the Indies. This was the company that sought to rival the East India Company by settling a colony in the New World; this was known as the Darien scheme. Other guild brethren were to be asked if they would join their stock to the Guildry's but whether any did so is not stated.[43] Two had bought shares privately as did another twenty-five merchants, one clergyman, one mariner, three professionals, two from the legal profession and eleven local government officials.[44] When the Equivalent was paid out, all that the

Guildry received back from this investment was £120 16s sterling, of which they had agreed in September 1707 to accept two-thirds in money and one third in Exchequer notes so that they could be paid 'presently'.[45] The private investors probably lost even more, as the Scottish parliament had passed an act in 1695 which reduced the risk to incorporations by protecting them from liability.[46]

The other major investment from which the Guildry certainly did not profit, was not initiated by them but encouraged by the council. This was the development of the Newport ferry, which will be described in chapter 9. They did occasionally lend to individuals despite their sixteenth-century decision. In the nineteenth century they moved their bank deposits depending on the amount of interest given but they did not seem to have lost much when banks closed in the town.

The incorporation was never very wealthy. In the sixteenth century, only about £38 Scots was paid for the gild silver which was quite an important part of their income. At the end of the seventeenth century, the income was £673 6s 2d Scots – just over £56 sterling.[47] In 1704-05, it had risen to £997 19s 10d Scots – just over £83 sterling. In each of these years interest on bonds from the town was counted, just over £132 Scots, even though it was noted as 'resting' since 1700 to 1704-05 (these accounts were not audited until September, 1706). By 1775-6, the charge and discharge amounted to £582 10s 5d sterling and this increased slightly to £654 7s 7d in 1779-80. The amount gained from dues for guild brothers for their freedom, for upsetting booths, mortcloths large and small, all varied from year to year, as did the expenditure and indeed apparently what the dean and collector chose to include. On the whole, however, there was income just enough to go to law to protect their privileges and most of the time, to give a modicum of assistance to their poorer members.

NOTES

[1]   D. Nicholas, *The Later Medieval City, 1300-1500* (London and New York, 1997), 59.

[2]   These acts are to be found fairly fully transcribed in Warden, *Burgh Laws*, 68ff.

[3] A.H. Millar (ed.), *The Compt Buik of David Wedderburne* (Edinburgh, 1898), xxiii, xxxi.

[4] M. Lynch (ed.), *The Oxford Companion to Scottish History* (Oxford, 2001), 384.

[5] A bag or sack of wool is now reckoned to have weighed 360lbs. R.D. Connor and A.D.C. Simpson, *Weights and Measures in Scotland, A European Perspective* (Edinburgh, 2004), 148.

[6] DCA; G1/1, f.6, 2-11-1570.

[7] DCA; G1/1, 3-10-1693.

[8] DCA; G1/2, 21-12-1697.

[9] DCA; G1/2, 23-4-1706.

[10] DTC, 26-7-1642.

[11] DTC, 15 and 22.5.1638.

[12] CRB, 7-7-1615.

[13] DCA; G1/1, f.25. 4-8-1591.

[14] DCA; G1/1, 17-12-1603.

[15] DCA; G1/2, 29-11-1712.

[16] DCA; G1/2, 14-8-1703.

[17] DCA; TC56/1, 13-8-1735.

[18] DCA; G1/2, 16-4-1706.

[19] DCA; G1/1, f.43, 22-6-1613.

[20] DCA; G1/1, f.46, 30-1-1616.

[21] DCA; G1/1, f.51.

[22] DCA; G1/1,2a, 8-9-1711.

[23] DCA; G1/1, f.39, 10-10-1609.

[24] DCA; G1/1, f.36, 17-1-1604.

[25] DCA; G1/1, f.38, 14-4-1607.

[26] DCA; G1/2, 7-2-1734.

[27] DCA; G1/2, 11-7-1738.

[28] DCA; G4/1, 22-10-1822.

[29] DCA; G1/5, 22-4-1822; 18-7-1822.

[30] DCA; G1/5, 29-9-1824.

[31] DCA; G4/1, 15-1-1825; G1/5, 18-11-1819.

[32] DCA; G1/1, f.91.

[33] DCA; G1/1, f.90.

[34] DCA; G1/1, ff.22, 23, 29-9-1588.

[35] DCA; G1/1, f.26.

[36] DCA; G1/1, f.42.

[37] DCA; G1/1, 1-9-1592.

[38] DCA; G3/1, Accounts, 1696-1751.

[39] DCA; G1/5, 6-12-1824.

[40] DCA; G1/7, 20-1-1854; G1/8. 24-11-1869.

[41] DCA; G1/1, f.34, 7-11-1598.

[42] DCA; G3/1, 2, 3, Accounts, 1696-1855.

[43] DCA; G1/1, 26-5-1696.

[44] W. Douglas Jones, 'The Bold Adventurers: A Quantitative Analysis of the Darien Subscription List (1696)', in *Scottish Economic & Social History*, 21 part one (2001), 28.

[45] DCA; G1/2, 6-9-1707, 13-9-1707.

[46] Douglas Jones, 35.

[47] DCA; G3/1, 1698-99.

5

THE RESPONSIBILITIES OF THE GUILDRY

Becoming a guild brother conferred privileges on individual merchants and on the Guildry as a whole but it also brought considerable responsibilities. The merchants had a considerable influence in the town. The presence of the dean, and after 1642, that of another guild member, on the town council gave undoubted gravitas. The council consulted it, especially on matters of taxation, trade and commerce, but there is some justification for the view that the Guildry in Scottish burghs was in effect a branch of local government.[1] For example, in 1739 the town had sent instructions to the MP John Drummond, and it was noted that it was the Guildry's duty to pass on their instructions in the same manner.[2] On the other hand before the Convention of Royal Burghs met, the Guildry made very firm proposals as to what the burgh's representative should bring up for discussion at that meeting. On another occasion the dean had the burgh's missive to the forthcoming Convention read out and when asked if there was anything they would have the commissioners 'to mynd … none answered anything'. But they were not usually so reticent.[3] The Guildry could also act as the agent for the Convention. In 1712, the assessors were asked to try to find out who were giving 'short valuations' in the burgh when the tax roll was being adjusted and to protest if they were finding any difficulty in ferreting out the necessary information.[4]

A few months after the parliamentary union, the value of their opinions on trade was illustrated when the Guildry court was convened on Saturday, 4 October 1707 to 'see what they had to inform' regarding trade to the new British parliament. Their suggestions included convoys guarded by cruisers for ships trading on the northern coasts of Britain, allowances for the import of iron, ensuring that herring was properly cured with the right sort of salt, and acts to regulate the linen trade.[5] They voiced opinions on matters varying from the 'insufficiency' of casks of Orkney butter in 1696, to more general dissatisfaction with the staple port at Campvere. The staple was a port where the country appointed a conservator who could help Scottish merchants and shippers there to cope with local regulations. The Dundee Guildry were prepared to discuss the proposal to move it to Rotterdam in 1668, and in 1699 to request that questions should be asked at the Edinburgh meeting about breaches of the staple regulations and accusations of maltreatment of merchants by the conservator.[6] Incidentally any action taken on the problems with Orkney butter cannot have been wholly successful for in 1701 the commissioners were asked once again to regulate its weight.[7] Another minor responsibility the Guildry bore when meetings of the Convention were held in Dundee was that they had to pay for 'dichting the hall'.

The standard of goods made or bought and sold, especially within the burgh, was also of concern to the merchants. Complaints about the quality of steel came to the fore in 1591. As this affected the Hammermen Trade particularly their deacon was consulted to help judge both the quality and how it could be improved. Merchants were warned not to sell foreign steel whether on its own or mixed with Scottish metal. Confiscation of all their wares plus a fine of 40s was threatened as the reputation of 'the whole estate' would be harmed by such practices. Cargoes of lintseed were regularly examined and at least one lot was refused until a much lower price than the seller had originally demanded was agreed – the examiners had found too much old seed in the batch. Wine too had to be carefully checked. One skipper and his crew were accused of spoiling wine they had carried from France by putting too many 'pluckes' on the barrels (plucks being small knobs marking the measure in a container). Perhaps the sailors had opened the barrels too often to check and perhaps sample the contents.

Textile manufacturing was such an important element in Dundee's economy that it would have been surprising not to find that this was a regular matter of concern to the Guildry. The linen trade grew rapidly in the eighteenth century and the Scottish government legislated to try ensure that linen yarn and cloth were properly made and used more by the lieges. From 1700 shrouds, for instance, were supposed to be made of linen rather than of wool.[8] In 1671 there was some agitation in the Guildry that the regulations made by both parliament and the Convention of Royal Burghs were not being observed 'to the great loss lieges susteyned'. The dean was instructed to write to magistrates in other burghs in Forfarshire, hoping to be able to meet them and agree about enforcing them.[9] A few years later an act of the council, which laid down rules for marking linen cloth sold in the burgh, was approved, and Thomas Butchard was appointed as 'visitor' – inspector – of both cloth and yarn.[10] A local merchant was also fined £100 because he had bought lint which had been refused when a Montrose merchant offered it to the Guildry and then removed it to Cottartown of Craigie. The offender was to remain in prison until he paid the large fine. Complaints by Dundee merchants who sold linen cloth in Perth that they were overtaxed were also heard sympathetically with letters being sent to the provost there; but the reaction from Perth is not known.[11]

In 1727 there were protests about retail sale of foreign lint or flax in the burgh by the English weights rather than by the Amsterdam. It was claimed that this was damaging to both the buyers and those who sold by the latter standard and it was to be announced 'by tuck of drum' the next day that the Amsterdam weight was to be used. This may seem odd, considering that all weights in the United Kingdom were supposed to be uniform after the Union of 1707 but the lint market was an international one and the rule may make sense if the goods came in packed and weighed according to foreign measures.[12]

A stampmaster was appointed in 1712 by the council,[13] and there had been concern among some Guildry members who lived in the Overgate and Murraygate that his office was to be established in the middle of the town. The council seem to have managed to persuade the authorities to set up two offices where he could examine cloth.[14]

When Charles White was appointed, he had to go to Edinburgh to see the Secretary for the Trustees for Improving Fisheries and Manufactures, bringing with him £100 sterling bail, and there receive his instructions and stamps (for which the Guildry meant to pay).[15] From 1732 the Guildry was also involved in trying to establish a bleachfield and the Trustees were prepared to assist, but they wanted to see the charges proposed. Negotiations went on all that year. The Trustees eventually offered a grant of £250 to assist with the estimated cost of over £838 with the condition that Guildry would find someone suitable to set up the field. The Guildry held out for £400 as they said their funds were too low for them to act otherwise.[16] This bid had apparently not succeeded for Trustees seem to have set up the bleach field themselves, as in 1739 a linen draper, Mr. Richard Holden of Baldovie – who had been mentioned initially as suitable to look after it the first season and teach the art of bleaching – asked to be recommended to the Trustees. He had proposals for whitening cloth at a much cheaper rate than had formerly been charged.[17]

The problem of piracy was a continual worry for traders. In the late sixteenth century the Convention of Royal Burghs had ordered that shippers who had had their goods spoiled by pirates should receive compensation from the burghs.[18] The effects of piracy and war on the linen trade particularly came up in 1739, when all the traders in Dundee petitioned parliament asking for protection against 'the insults and robberies of the Spanish in the West Indies'. As linen was the 'principal branch of business in this place' they felt that their shipping and trade should be succoured.[19] In 1824 they were once again sending a petition to parliament regarding linen, this time in competition with hemp, asking for adjustment of taxes on hempen goods so that local manufacturers could still compete with foreigners. In what seemed an unusually honest response the chancellor replied that he was aware of the problem but it would be difficult to assist without diminishing the revenue![20]

The wool trade was also an important part of the Dundee economy and the Guildry had influence here too. Even the Duke of Atholl was prepared to accept their decision on the size and quality of plaids to be sold at Kirkmichael market.[21] Here the Guildry had to deal with fears of competition which might affect the local trade. A factory had been built to make wool cloth, presumably that at Newmills, but by 1689 the Dundee Guildry at least was protesting that the quality of the cloth made was poor and the cost exorbitant.[22] Worse still, it was said that the makers were importing English cloth and selling it as their own. The provost, as commissioner to the Convention of Royal Burghs, was to bring this up at the next meeting in Perth and also to support the Dean of Guild's court's powers to deal with this.[23]

Maintaining the quality of goods sold either privately or in the market was the responsibility of several officials whose appointment was in the hands of the Guildry. For instance two men became 'apprisers' or 'visitors' of sheepskins. Their duty was to value fleeces at the market and also to make sure they were in good condition. A glover or a flesher would have been the obvious candidate for such a job and in 1740, Andrew Procter, a glover, and Samuel Mathers, a flesher, were indeed appointed but on occasion apprisers were simply described as merchants. Another such position was that of the common 'metster' or 'metter', the man responsible for measuring goods and land for sale. He served the whole community and was really a council servant but it was the Guildry who appointed him. While there is no indication of when nominating sheepskin apprisers became the responsibility of the Guildry, we know the first date and the reason for decision to create the post of metster. In November 1593 it emerged that there had been 'great abuse' in the measuring of cloth and other merchandise. The resulting 'questions, debaites and contraversies' between buyers and sellers were 'to the slander of this burgh and all honest merchants'. To remedy the situation the new metster was to measure all cloth and plaiding bought and sold in Dundee. He was to be paid 8d for each 100 ells of single plaiding or narrow cloth, which had to be recouped from the seller immediately after the measuring. If a merchant measured his own, he had to report to the metster and pay the same prices. A fine of £2 was imposed on any guild brother who did not voluntarily show the collector the cloth, as well as pay the usual dues to the metster.[24]

Then there were the distributors of 'smiddy coal'. In 1554 the town council had found it necessary to restrict the amount the inhabitants could buy. Like so many laws at the time, these were easier to make than to enforce. Attempts were made at several times to regulate where coal was to be unloaded and the amount each person could buy, and two deacons were appointed to take note of coal boats and the amount delivered. In 1605 the dean was authorised to measure the creels used to carry coal to customers.[25] In 1609 the Guildry contributed their share in trying to control the market, when two guild brethren were made distributors to prevent the abuses by speculators – 'sum privat persons' – who were buying whole loads and selling them on at a high profit. The distributors were empowered to buy the whole shipload, except what the smiths of the Hammerman Trade needed for their work; their forges obviously needed more than the normal household. The town bell was to ring to announce the imminent arrival of a boat with smiddy coal and the distributors had to deliver it in bolls to all who had it ordered before it was unloaded. Payment had to be made on the spot.[26]

All these officials, apprisers, and smiddy coal distributors, were appointed on the same day as the dean and Guildry officers were elected. While there were always town councillors present on these occasions, either in their official capacity or as guild brethren, the Guildry's importance in the commerce and trade of the burgh is illustrated in their responsibility in dealing with such appointments and in making such rules about the ways in which trading was carried out. The presence of such officers and the existence of such rules were important for the confidence of buyers and sellers alike.

Indeed, one of the most important functions of the Guildry was that of ensuring that all weights and measures used for selling and buying goods in the town were correct. The local weights which were in the Guildry's custody were checked against the national weights which the Scottish parliament attempted to standardise at various times. In February 1512 for instance, the Great Chamberlain of Scotland had decided to alter some of the standard weights. The change, however, could not be instantaneous and in March, the magistrates and community of Dundee were given permission to use the old ones in their custody without fear of prosecution, until the new 'mettis, wechtis and mesouris' were made and delivered to them.[27] After 1661 the standard weights against which all others were supposed to be checked were the responsibility of various burghs – the ell, the measurement of cloth in Edinburgh: the stone in Lanark: the joug, the pint for liquid measures, in Stirling: the firlot for dry goods in Linlithgow. Other burghs had to send their weights and measures to be checked against the standards, so periodically the Guildry had to arrange for a messenger to take theirs to the appropriate burgh.

All burgesses were legally permitted to keep in their own houses elwands – rods of one ell length for measuring cloth – and weights which had to be stamped with the burgh seal. The Guildry's duty was to test the privately owned against those in their custody. In November 1570 the dean and his officer were authorised to go through the burgh four times a year and examine all weights and measures in use. Any which did not conform to the town's 'common stone' were to be broken and the offender fined 8s for the first offence and £5 for the second. Anyone who was found guilty of using faulty measures a third time was to lose his liberty as a freeman for ever.[28]

On 18 February 1612 John White, or Whittet, who was found guilty of using too small measures was fined £20. As others at the same time had been using only one or two faulty weights, the total fines imposed added £47 3s 4d to the Guildry's coffers, but White's offence must have been deemed much greater. The suspicion must be that he was suspected of deliberate cheating for he was threatened with banishment from the burgh if he offended again – a threat that was not applied to any of the others on the list.[29] Two years later a woman was named for a second time among those with faulty weights. Margaret Fyff was fined £7 Scots as her iron one pound weight was four drops short, and her brass weight light by three drops (a drop being one sixteenth of an ounce). She had been convicted before and was paying dearly for repeating the offence – or perhaps of having never corrected her weights – as only two days before her conviction 40 pence had been decided on as the fine for each drop short of the correct weight. A century later, in 1705, the dean was instructed to correct any faulty weights and charge owners £40 Scots for each drop short of the town's standard weights – which was a substantial increase.[30]

The inaccuracy of privately owned weights and measures was discussed in 1613.[31] It was suggested that the reason for the large number failing the tests might be that they were made of stones and lead. Setting a prospective fine of £10 for disobeying new regulations, the Guildry laid down that in future no merchants of Dundee were to buy or sell by any weights unless they were of troy weight and were made of iron or brass, both materials less susceptible to illegal alterations. To assist those who might have had difficulty in paying the cost of replacing their old weights the treasurer, William Guthrie, had already procured some iron weights which he would sell for £5. A month later, wine containers which were 'found disagreeable with the joug' were to be broken and users fined. In May of the following year, sellers of small wine – retailers rather than wholesalers – beer, ale and other drinks were ordered to bring in the 'stoupis', their flagons or decanters or mugs, to be stamped with the town's stamp or risk a £10 fine. Goods sold in bulk like grain or smiddy coals had to be measured in containers equal to the Linlithgow measure.

Checking that the Dundee merchants were maintaining their integrity demanded constant care. For instance, despite the attempts to make all weights of metal in 1613, in September 1614 the order had to be repeated that all stone weights should be broken. Even measuring sticks could be faulty. In 1700 the dean and his court prohibited the use of any linen elwand not sealed at the ends and stamped with the town's seal; a ten-merk fine was imposed quite apart from any punishment the magistrates might like to inflict. Linen cloth was such a vital part of Dundee's economy that it is hardly surprising to find that the town council might take a hand in dealing with offenders. However, the Guildry still had the responsibility of keeping the measures correct and they ruled that the ends of elwands should be sealed by their officer in presence of their collector, the officer to be paid a fee of ten pennies Scots.[32] Another type of problem arose in 1649. Faulty weights had been found but no fine could be imposed; the owner could not be identified as these had been lost at the storming of the town in 1645.[33]

Fault did not always lie with the traders, however. In 1831 there were complaints about the Guildry's own officer, William Roger, who was accused of seizing quantities of butter which he had declared were underweight. He was proved wrong, but he still failed to return all of it to the rightful owners. On other occasions when he seized butter or declared it was underweight, it was claimed that he did not take enough time, that his coat sleeve interfered with the tongue, the pointer of the balance, and that he had been holding the balance in such a way which must have affected the weight shown.[34] The Guildry were sufficiently impressed by the witnesses and sacked him.

The weight of bread was a very important matter to the population as a whole as it was a vital part of their diet. In 1730 a committee was appointed to inspect the weight of the Dundee bakers' bread when the dean asked for this, but there seems to have been some doubt about whether they had the right to do so. In the sixteenth century the bakers and the town council had been at odds over bread weights and prices,[35] and in 1738 there was some consultation with Edinburgh about whether the price claimed by the Dundee bakers would have been allowed there. In March 1821 the dean and his assessors expressed grave doubts about whether in fact it was part of their duties, or if it had ever been the practice for them to examine bread for weight, or to seize and condemn any that was deficient. They informed the provost that they had thought they had better return all the seized loaves to the owners.[36] In 1826, however, the Guildry decided to regulate the weight of bread by producing the loaf-shaped bronze weights shown in Plate 11.

After the 1707 union of the parliaments a further complication arose for the Guildry in the business of controlling weights and measures. These were supposed to become uniform over the whole of Great Britain but it took a long time for that to be achieved. The dean had received British standard weights and measures in September 1708 and a proclamation was made all round the town announcing that after 1 November of that year no others were to be used.[37] This was a vain hope. Five years later in 1712, the Guildry called on the Dundee commissioners to the Convention of Royal Burghs to try to persuade the members to order lintseed measures to be made the same in all burghs.[38] And how effective that was we can surmise by the fact that in 1750, the Dundee and Perth Guildries were consulting about which measure they would use.[39] The Perth Guildry had resolved to sell by the Linlithgow measure and wrote to ask what the practice was in Dundee. The Dean of Guild's Court decided to follow the Perth example and sent notices round the town immediately as the next day was 3 April, market day. Ten months later £20 sterling was the fine for offending. The Linlithgow measure was recognised at that point as being 21 pints 1 mutchkin in the firlot. The Scots pint was equal to three imperial pints, and the mutchkin was one quarter of the Scots pint. The firlot was the measure of capacity for various goods like grain and coal but was not the same for each. Older Scottish weights and measures varied from burgh to burgh and pose considerable problems of interpretation in some economic situations. They were not always made locally and one of the Dundee measures which survives was made in Nuremberg in 1672 by G.B. Weinmann.[40]

Government officials were as much under the Guildry's authority as anyone else where weights and measures were concerned. A Dundee merchant, Thomas Ogilvy, accused James Tennant, a landwaiter (a customs officer), of using weights which were too heavy, when he was assessing tobacco for export in 1735. One of the bailies, John Jobson, tested Tennant's weights against those of the government which were in the town's custody. It emerged that they were 8lb 8oz 12 drops overweight in all, one alone contributing 2lb 5oz 3 drops to this excess – a difference which would have added substantially to a merchant's costs. Unfortunately there is no mention of whether the landwaiter had to pay for his mistake or whether it was considered deliberate or accidental.[41] As late as June 1826 the Customs House weights were again discovered to be faulty when a flax spinner, sending flax by sea from Dundee, found that the government weights did not correspond with those in his warehouse.[42]

The financial cost of having charge of the town's weights was not light, though there was compensation to the Guildry's funds from the fines paid by cheats. The weights needed regular repairs and this is shown in the accounts throughout the period when the incorporation bore that responsibility. Wood measures decayed and while lead, iron and brass were hardier, they suffered from oxidisation. Inevitably too, constant handling wore them down. Keeping a salt measure in good condition must have been specially expensive, because of the corrosive effect of salt on metal. In the 1661-62 accounts it is listed that three new ones were bought for over £5, repairs to older weights were also needed: 16s to mend only one. The accounts of 1663-64 show that £7 12s was needed for iron work and in 1669 more weights had to be replaced at a cost of £14. The next year, the bill for weights (unspecified) and a pair of scales was £19, and brands were also necessary to stamp containers whose weight had been tested and confirmed.

In March 1820, by which time the Guildry and town finances had been completely separated, the Guildry still bore this responsibility. The dean called a special meeting to take an inventory of all the weights and measures in the Guildry's possession and to test the new ones lately made by order of the dean and assessors.[43] It is a very long list, including beams, English weights, bell handled and flat, from drops to half-hundredweights, bread weights for quartern and half quartern loaves – despite the doubts expressed about the Guildry's duties regarding bread – liquid measures from mutchkins to gallons and wine containers, some in brass and some in wood, hooped with copper. Corn and coals also had to provided for. There were brands, sieves for testing meal, rollers for striking measures, a hand barrow and the list also included some articles 'not in use', such as Dutch weights, a deficient Troy weight and a Linlithgow bushel.

By the early nineteenth century the increase in trade in the burgh laid a far greater burden on the Guildry than ever before as they struggled to maintain standards. In December 1817 they advertised that the dean and assessors were determined to enforce the burgh laws and would be inspecting the weights, but in 1819 they required the assistance of the town's officers who were each paid one guinea for their services. The government realised that action was needed to achieve standardisation and in 1825 a new act was passed to that end.[44] It caused some friction locally between Guildry and council as it now made the town custodian of the weights, but the new act had not removed the dean's jurisdiction. The incorporation also made the point that they had always paid their officer as custodian of all the weights.

In 1832, however, when the dean's judicial powers were removed and vested in the council by the act of 1831, necessary to set up a council after its disenfranchisement, the dean and assessors decided in September that they could no longer bear the expense of maintaining the various measures, and these were offered to the council.[45] It was also suggested that the council should begin to rent the officer's shop where he kept all the necessary equipment and also pay part of his salary.[46] The town agreed to pay £45 for the weights actually used, to take over the rent of the shop and agree with the officer about his salary. Alexander Kay suggested that the old weights should also be bought by the council and preserved as ancient relics,[47] and it was proposed that all the old tin measures still in the incorporation's custody should be given to the various charities in the town.[48] So ended one important public duty of Guildry in which there can be no doubt that in this role they acted carefully and conscientiously for many centuries.

NOTES

[1]   Murray, *Early Burgh Organisation*, i, 464.

[2]   DCA; TC/1, 21-11-1739.

[3]   DCA; G1/1, 1-7-1693.

[4]   DCA; G1/2, 27-6-1712.

[5]   DCA; G1/2, 4-10-1707.

[6]   DCA; G1/1, 5-7-1696, 27-10-1668.

[7]   DCA; G1/2, 28-6-1701.

[8]   DCA; G3/2, Anonymous typed article on mortcloths.

[9]   Warden, 155.

[10] Warden, 159.

[11] Warden, 162.

[12] DCA; G1/2, 3-10-1727.

[13] DCA; DTC, 5-8-1712.

[14] DCA; DTC, 11-11-1712.

[15] DCA; G1/2, 8-11-1727.

[16] DCA; G1/2, November and December 1732.

[17] DCA; G1/2, 21-11-1739, 22-11-1739.

[18] DCA; G1/1, f.18.

[19] DCA; G1/2, 28-2-1739.

[20] DCA; G1/5, 13-3-1824.

[21] DCA; G1/2, 17-6-1706.

[22] H. Hamilton, *Economic History of Scotland in the Eighteenth Century* (Oxford,1963), 131-132.

[23] Warden, 164.

[24] DCA; G1/1, f.29, 5-11-1593.

[25] Maxwell, *History of Old Dundee*, 62-64.

[26] DCA; G1/1, f.40, 31-10-1609. The boll varied in weight and volume over the centuries and also for different commodities.

[27] Connor, *Weights and Measures*, 272-3.

[28] DCA; G1/1, November 1570.

[29] DCA; G1/1, f.45.

[30] DCA; G1/2, 21-7-1705.

[31] DCA; G1/1, f.44.

[32] DCA; G1/2, 8-8-1700.

[33] DCA; G1/1, f. 96.

[34] DCA; G1/6, September 1831.

[35] Maxwell, *History of Old Dundee*, 93-98.

[36] DCA; G1/5, 5-3-1821; Letter to Provost David Brown, 6-3-1821.

[37] DCA; DTC, 16-9-1708.

[38] DCA; G1/2, 27-12-1712.

[39] DCA; TC56/3, f42.

[40] Connor, *Weights and Measures*, 329, 467.

[41] DCA; G1/2, 7-7-1735.

[42] DCA; G4/1, 110.

[43] DCA; G1/5, 9-3-1820.

[44]   5 G.IV. c.14.
[45]   DCA; G1/6, 18-9-1832.
[46]   DCA; G1/6, 10-11-1832.
[47]   DCA; G1/6, 10-11-1832.
[48]   DCA; G1/6, 9-1-1833.

6

CHARITY

The care of the poor and the sick, those who were known as the 'decayed' members, was considered an important duty by most societies formed by men with similar interests. So it was with the Dundee Guildry for most of its history, although it is perhaps surprising that it was not until 1570 that the Dundee Guildry decided to set up a special fund for this purpose.[1] The dean, Alexander Scrymgeour, and ten others met in the council-house on 13 November of that year to consider the estate of the 'common voice of the merchants'. It was deplored that there was at that time no 'common good' fund for either the defence of the merchants' liberties or support for their 'decayed brethren'.

The decision to remedy this state of affairs may have been a sign of this new broom, Alexander Scrymgeour, trying to set the Guildry's house in order. The meeting ordained that for three years the dean, or his factor with the dean's authority, should be able to levy contributions to set up such a fund. Every merchant in the burgh was to pay six groats for each stick (bale) of cloth and four groats for every bag of any other goods. Abroad, in France, Venice, 'Queensbridge' (Königsberg) and 'all other places', similar taxes were to be paid on salmon, herring, hides and skins of shearling and goats, white leather and cloth. All this without any damage to any 'old letters or privilege'.

These funds were obviously expected to be extra beyond any allowed in the Merchants' Letter, for example, or any other fees that were due to the Guildry. Care of poor or sick guild brothers or of their families was not mentioned in 1515 but from this later date it was a constant and important part of the activities of the incorporation.

In January 1584 the dean, his assessors and all the merchants met to reaffirm their rules, particularly regarding dealings with unfreemen but at the end of the meeting the question of help for their poor members was dealt with. Times were obviously rather harder than they had been some years before. It was remarked that there had been great changes and expenses daily falling on the merchants as they tried to defend their liberties and supported their sick and poor – 'charges far above that they in times before wold have done the same'. The dean and his assessors were exhorted to be diligent in collecting all the money due to the Guildry. The fees were all increased; for example £5 was to be charged for upsetting booths, compared to £2 in 1576 except in the case of the sons of burgesses who would pay 20s.[2] It was apparently not too easy to make sure that all the fees, etc. reached the Guildry. In 1585 when the collector, Walter Hay, produced his accounts for 1580-1583, resting (owing) £102 7s 2d, there was a note of the damage done to the society because he had not been able to obtain all the money due. The general funds were used to provide pensions and in 1676, for example, £76 16s 8d had been paid out. Pensioners continued to receive varying amounts. In 1693-4 a total of £62 18s 8d was doled out; £91 14s 8d was spent in 1695, some receiving 12s 3d per week, some 6s 8d, others being paid £1 4s by the month, the last in 1693-4 to widows. Another entry for this year was 'also by the provost and dean of guild's order to William Scrope at several times £5 16s'.

It is perhaps worth mentioning here that the dean had a certain amount of discretion with regard to the funds. All through the seventeenth century and beyond entries record donations 'by the dean's order', one in 1702-3 for instance for £5 16s to 'two Orkneymen taken by the French'. An interesting donation was mentioned in the 1706-7 accounts, also ordered by the dean – £1.9s to a German Protestant, Mr. Constantin.[3] Sometimes deans, not only in Dundee, contributed from their own funds: Aberdeen deans were renowned for their generosity.[4] One Dundee dean, James Fairweather, offered to do without his salary providing that the court enacted that no future dean should be paid until the Guildry was in better condition.[5]

In 1701-2 when times were very hard, £180 16s was paid out in poor relief from a total income of £607 15s 2d. It is perhaps not surprising to find the dean in November 1702 reporting that the stock of the Guildry was exhausted by the pensions and he desired the court to hold them under consideration until the next court day – but nothing seemed to be done then. It was 1705 before a committee was appointed to 'revise' the Guildry's finances and report how much they could pay in pensions.[6] In 1708 at a meeting convened to consider making additions to the revenue, it would appear that after overtures from the council suggesting that maltmen apprentices should be entered by the Guildry, the fees of 40s paid by these boys were to be so used. The additional income arising from this source does not seem to have been very effective for in 1709 it emerged that no pensions had been paid for several years. As there was now a balance the dean asked if he could renew payments and this was agreed. Things were worse again in 1713 when the collector, David James, declared that he was 'very uneasie in his office' and refused again to pay pensions, as he had no money. The dean informed him that he must not even pay the stipends without his order.[7]

One interesting addition to the poor relief fund was organised in 1723. One merchant, John Barclay, had bought lint from Riga and offered it to the Guildry for them to have first refusal, as was the correct practice. This load was not wanted at the time and Barclay was allowed to sell it as well as he could, but he had to pay 3% of all he gained from the sale to the poor fund.[8]

Those eligible for help from the Guildry's funds were fairly restricted. Full members who fell on hard times qualified, as did their widows and orphans. Once differing classes of membership were offered with different entry dues, one which gave benefits to a guild brother's family after his death, the other which was less expensive, for a member for his lifetime only, only he could claim a pension. As a lifetime member a man could benefit from all the privileges that membership conveyed while he was alive, but had not bought what was in effect an insurance policy for his wife and children. In 1737, one maltman, Robert Tod, had to beg for a return of the 40 merks he had paid for permission to set up his stall as he was now very poor.

He gave up any interest his children could claim so he was repaid his capital sum.[9] Non-residents too were often refused relief, though there were exceptions: in 1705 for instance when it was stated in the accounts that some of the pensioners were 'out of town'.[10]

Monetary aid was not the only method of relieving poverty and want and throughout the whole time the Guildry helped its poorer brethren and their families. For instance in 1710 the dean was instructed to keep in hand £20 of the funds to buy coal in the case of scarcity, which would then be sold to members probably at less than the cost. Within a few days it was realised that this sum was not nearly enough and the dean was authorised to buy twenty chalders – a measure that varied according to what commodity was being bought or sold – first using the £20 and then borrowed money if it was needed.[11] Assistance with funeral costs was another form of aid when, for example, in 1818 £1 sterling was given to help one member's family.[12]

When bread was the staple diet the cost of grain affected the price of living drastically. Regularly meal was bought when food was scarce, with the provision that no-one was to be allowed to buy it in order to sell for profit. In 1729 a committee was set up to prepare a scheme for providing for the poor during times of scarcity. It had been suggested by several members that meal should be bought at bargain prices to be ready for such occasions.[13] Though nothing seems to have resulted at this time, in 1740, action was taken after poor harvests when food was very scarce and expensive. It was thought that £5 yearly might be added to the pension fund but more substantial aid was needed. In August of that year the dean, George Lyon, reported that families in the burgh had no meal. He was authorised to sell as much of any in the Guildry's possession as he thought proper, at a price of 11d per peck but at only 10d to the poorest. Later in December of that year, the Guildry decided to buy 400 bolls of the 1740 crop at £9 Scots per boll from Mr. Troup, but accepted his offer of 450 bolls at £8 per boll. This was to be stored in a girnel (granary) and a committee of eight was appointed to oversee its distribution – a quorum being four with the dean as ever always one of these four.

Nothing more was said on this occasion about storage but in 1752 when 500 quarters of peas and beans had been shipped to Dundee, the Guildry paying the prime cost, the Guildry Court offered the shipper, Alex Murray, the use of the west room in the town house, at that time the Guild Hall, and of rooms in the hospital or where spare space could be found.[14] A few days later, however, Provost Yeaman suggested that a warehouse should be taken and used as a girnel as long as it was needed.[15]

All the Dundee institutions worked together when times were really hard for the poor in the town. In the 1740s the kirk session and the Dundee trades combined to help feed the starving and the Guildry was approached to join with the session in buying peas and beans from London to support those in want. This was agreed to unanimously and arrangements had to be made about the purchasing of the food, its insurance in transit, its storage when it arrived, and commission to the merchant acting for them. The merchant in London was not satisfied with the terms offered. He wanted immediate payment of the whole sum due him, not just the interest which was all that had first been offered, and means had to be found to raise the amount needed (900 quarters had been ordered, one quarter being eight bushels).[16] As it was thought too risky to bring such a large amount in one ship, two were to be freighted.[17] In April 1741 there was an attempt to freight a vessel to go to Holland where the grain was considered best, if the kirk session agreed to share in the bargain, and the dean had this arranged by the next day. On this occasion it was oatmeal that was ordered. Pulses bought had to be made into meal when flour from corn was not available, which meant that a mealmaker had to be employed at further expense. John Ballantain, a Dundee mealmaker, undertook the work at 8s 6d per week. Distribution was the responsibility of a committee who issued billets in the town house to all wanting a share. Without such a voucher no meal was handed over.

The whole exercise was a considerable strain on the finances of all the public bodies in Dundee. In March 1741 William Peatrie of London wrote that he was still owed £300 sterling, and he wondered how he was to be paid. All the committee could do was to give security and agree they would pay as soon as possible. The dean had to borrow £50 from Bailie Jobson and from James Ramsay to make some payment, but when the ship arrived and needed someone to inspect the unloading there was more money needed. The previous collector had to be asked what balance there was so that freight and other charges could be paid: and the chilling comment – if there was none, it had to be borrowed. The charity of individuals is not part of the Guildry's records but it is worth noting that George Dempster, the Dundee merchant, a member who was charged with forestalling meal at one point, offered the Guildry and kirk session a quantity of beans at the price it had cost him, an offer which was thankfully received.

Dundee did not suffer alone at this time and also did not fail to give what assistance was possible to neighbouring burghs. A Forfar merchant wrote that supplies there were 'too bere' and that if some could be sent he would undertake to replace it whenever the supplies which he had ordered did arrive. Kirriemuir's minister sent word that that burgh was in great straits and 5 bolls of peas and beans were sent off on the same terms as those granted to Forfar. Fortunately the next harvest was better and that crisis passed, but poverty was an abiding problem. The poor were always there.

A few years previously, in 1738, the town council had recommended that a fund should be set up, to which the Guildry would contribute, to build a workhouse where beggars and other poor in Dundee would be employed. This was a considerable innovation in Scotland where outdoor relief was the usual method of providing for the poor. Thirty-five members including the provost and two bailies attended the meeting of the Guildry Court considering this proposal and agreed to a contribution. The Guildry's funds – its 'stock' – were to be inspected by one committee which was to meet any other which might be set up to decide on how to finance such a workhouse and report back. Further any guild brethren who were also members of the kirk session were to inform that body of what the Guildry Court had decided and to desire that the church funds should also be examined to see what they could give.[18] Other societies had joined in the scheme and in January 1739 the Guildry had agreed to contribute £10; the Masons £2 2s; the Slaters £1; and the Maltmen £5 – all in sterling and all for one year.[19] The following month the Dean presented to a full meeting of his court the town council's proposal that a tax of 6% on all household rents in the burgh should be set and by June 1739 this had been agreed by the dean, members of his court and several other inhabitants of the burgh. Perhaps as a result of the imposition of this general tax, in November 1739 the Guildry's particular contribution had been reduced to £5. However, in 1752 the committee of the Guildry council and the kirk session were still discussing the question and they agreed unanimously that a poorhouse was the proper way of maintaining the poor, with a salary of £25 for the overseer. The Guildry had to point out that, if this was too much for their funds, they could grant no additional pensions until their stock recovered.[20]

This had been a somewhat disingenuous move on the part of the council. After the Guildry gained full control of its finances several matters saw the light of day which had hitherto been concealed in the obscurity of the town's accounts. In 1819 a Guildry committee discovered a bond and deed dated 1731 and 1734 which had been recorded in the burgh court books. One, James Ramsay, had endowed the council with 2000 merks for the purpose of building a workhouse for 'containing idle and vagrant persons as well men as women'. The patrons controlling this were to be the provost, a bailie, the dean and the convener of the Nine Trades. If the patrons failed the members of the Dean of Guild's Court were to become overseers. The first purchase with this money was to be a field for the workhouse and utensils for the work with which the inmates would be employed, neither of which could be alienated from their original purpose.

It was discovered that the sum in Ramsay' mortification had been lent to the town in a bond of 24 September 1734 but no bond could be found. In 1743 the factor for this account had lifted interest due and lent it to private individuals, a process which continued, and the sum in the account had increased to £2,241 17s 4d. That same year the town gained Ramsay's consent to pay £100 Scots to George Mark, a teacher of mathematics, until the workhouse was erected. There had apparently been a workhouse in 1754 and the hospital was also used for that purpose. The patrons of the mortification had used the interest to support it but by Whitsunday 1757 it appears to have been given up. Not surprisingly the committee thought the patrons had failed in their duty and the Guildry could take over the money available to build a workhouse. The general meeting to which this was reported thoroughly approved of the conclusions and it was proposed that several people who had been lent money from the mortfication, including the late dean Patrick Whitson and Bailie David Brown, should be asked to repay the money lent from the fund, with interest.[21] However, the town seems to have managed to retain control and the dean was still only one of the patrons in the late nineteenth century.[22]

The Guildry's finances were often stretched by the needs of their pensioners and in 1831 the dean and assessors were horrified to learn there was an excess of expenditure of £115 12s 8d over income, with pensioners having been paid £191 2s 8d.[23] As there were statutory demands on their funds such as their contribution to the ministers' stipends, money could not be paid out to their poor with gay abandon. Claims had always been given serious consideration but in the nineteenth century, with the Guildry alone responsible for their expenditure, they were even more closely scrutinised. After 1818 it appears that sons of members were not granted permanent pensions. One woman lost hers when it emerged that her husband had opened a grocer's shop in North Castle Street, while a shoemaker's petition was refused because he had a property in the Overgate.[24] In 1838 the dean and his assessors announced that all pensioners were to be notified that pensions would be paid on 2 December in the town hall. This was to give the committee responsible for allotting them the opportunity to see all those benefiting personally, unless they were too ill to appear.

Another method of relieving poverty was what one might term self-help by the poor themselves – begging. Attempts were made to regulate the demands of beggars by licensing them, usually to beg in their own parishes. In 1777 it appeared that the methods used in Dundee were not working. The town council had asked the Guildry and other societies in the burgh to consult together to try to improve matters. They had met repeatedly and proposed a legal assessment by which contributions could be collected, and the aim was to provide for the begging poor in their own homes.[25]

The cooperation between the various societies in the town towards the poorest sections of their community has been illustrated by such activities as their joint purchasing of meal and the building of the workhouse. The whole burgh was also involved on other occasions: for instance, in the winter of 1800-1801 money was raised by public subscription for the immediate relief of the poor of the parish. In April 1801, despite what was described as the 'liberal contributions' of the inhabitants and significantly of 'others', supplies were nearly exhausted and the Guildry generously sent an extra £100 from their own funds to the Committee for the Relief of the Poor.[26]

The status of the incorporation as a charitable society was discussed by a committee which organised the Guildry's poor fund in 1819.[27] Their conclusions must have come as a shock to the many members who joined in hope of some help in the case of their infirmity or poverty in old age. It was stated firmly that the committee thought the Guildry associated for the protection of their mutual rights as a Trade; their funds were therefore applicable only for that purpose, defence of their privileges and the prosecution of measures which may be deemed useful to the society. The members of this committee surely did not know about the decision of November 1570, which had never been revoked, or if they did they perhaps decided to ignore it. The committee may have been trying to protect the incorporation from excess demands of relief from the funds, for their comment was palliated by the following statement that they highly approved of the plan adopted for granting to reduced members a part of the annual revenue, subject always to control and superintendence by the Dean and his assessors. It was also emphasized that no-one without Guildry connections could be given assistance.

With revenue of £350 per annum and £130 due in permanent expenses, only £220 was left for general use. The preceding year had seen £160 allotted to pensions and no increase was possible. The list of pensioners was reviewed and of the twenty-six names on the current list, some were to be struck off, for various reasons such as being non-residents. However, as in earlier times Dundonians who had moved away from the town were sometimes made allowances. For instance John Soutar, living in Glasgow, received an allowance in September 1837 and in 1858, 2s was paid each month to Dr. David Greig on behalf of a widow in Birmingham. Of fifteen new claimants one was written off as he was getting money from the Seamen's Fraternity. There was to be greater insistence on claimants` producing proof of their rights. It was also decided to discover if other towns paid non-residents. In 1823 a rather unpleasant light was thrown on the attitude of some of more fortunate to those who had fallen in hard times. It was suggested that pensioners should not be allowed to vote in any matters at general meetings. Fortunately for the Guildry's reputation this proposal was thrown out.[28]

In 1867 the incorporation received a substantial increase to their poor fund. Edward Baxter, one of the family of manufacturers who were considerable benefactors to the town in various ways, presented the Guildry with £2,000 in shares in the North Eastern Railway Company to help provide relief of the poor of the society. It was decided to keep a separate account book, showing precisely how these funds were used.[29] This was duly done with the collector having to report on how these funds stood. This involved so much work for him that in 1868 he was awarded an increase of £5 to his salary. Despite the generosity of the Baxter Mortification or Bequest, the needs of the poor and the number of applicants were so numerous at that time that in September 1868 only 2s per month was all that was available.[30] Ten years later the North East Railway Company informed the Guildry that they meant to exercise their powers to redeem the preference shares in which the capital was invested. The Dean and his assessors accepted payment of £2,000 in cash and looked for another investment.

Whatever the doubts expressed about the legality of the Guildry's spending on their poor and disabled, pensions to poor or sick members or their families continued into the twentieth century.

The individual sums handed out were small as the incorporation's revenue was never large, but the certainty of even 4s or 5s each month must have been very welcome to many recipients. In the nineteenth century too, extra payments were made in the winter months: an extra 1s in 1860, and in December 1863, an extra 4s 6d was authorised for each pensioner for the next three months.[31]

By the end of the twentieth century there were no guild brothers or their dependants in need of personal assistance and the Guildry now use the funds available for charity for other purposes such as awards to various colleges in the town or to restoration of buildings, both aspects of the burgh's life which were among the Guildry's earlier interests.[32] One example of the type of help given to the community was for instance the presentation in June 2001 of travel scholarships to graduate students in the School of Town and Regional Planning at the University of Dundee.[33] By such means the Guildry's connections with various aspects of Dundee life and their attempts to benefit its inhabitants is still maintained.

NOTES

[1]   DCA; G1/1, f.6.

[2]   DCA; G1/1, ff.7,19.

[3]   DCA; G3/1, 1706-7.

[4]   R.E. Tyson 'Poverty and Poor Relief', in *Scottish Archives*, 8 (2002), 35.

[5]   DCA; G1/2, 3.12.1722.

[6]   DCA; G1/2, 1-11-1702, 30-6-1705.

[7]   DCA; G1/2, 10-12-1713.

[8]   DCA; G1/2, 30-5-1723.

[9]   DCA; G1/2 , 200.

[10]   DCA; G3/1, 1705-6 accounts, audited 1708.

[11]   DCA; G1/2, 21-6-1710, 26-6-1710.

[12]   DCA; G1/5, 12-12-1818.

[13]   DCA; G1/2, 8-3-1729.

[14]   DCA; G1/2, 14-3-1752.

[15]   DCA; G1/2, 18-3-1752.

16   Connor, *Weights and measures*, 211.
17   G1/2, August 1740-April 1741.
18   DCA; G1/2, 23-12-1738; TC56/1.
19   DCA; TC56/1, 18-1-1739.
20   DCA; TC56/2, 30-3-1752.
21   DCA; G1/5, 13-10-1819.
22   Warden, 225.
23   DCA; G1/6, 7-3-1832.
24   DCA; G1/6, 325; G1/5, 31-5-1827.
25   DCA; G1/4, 1777. The volume is fire-damaged, so the exact date is not clear.
26   DCA; G3/2, 1800-1801; G1/4 10-4-1801.
27   DCA; G1/5, 13-7-1819.
28   DCA; G1/5, 26-10-1823.
29   DCA; G1/8.
30   DCA; G1/8, 30-9-1868.
31   DCA; G1/7, 1860; December, 1863.
32   Goodfellow, *Guildry of Dundee*, v.
33   University of Dundee Press Release.

Plate 1

The Town House of Dundee by William Adam (opened in 1734),
showing the 'Gilderyroom' on the west and the 'Council House' on
the east; these were later interchanged. The Guildry ceased
occupying their room when the Town House was demolished and
the New Council Chambers in Crichton Street became available in
the 1920s.

Plate 2

The West Chamber of the Town House, originally the Guildry
Room then used by the Town Council.

Plate 3

Many of the Guildry's earlier records were destroyed or badly
damaged in the Town House fire of 1909. Some of the charred
pages, like these, were restored in the 1960s.

Plate 4

Detail of a Guildry banner depicting the 4XX symbol. Versions of
this symbol have been found throughout Western Europe from as
early as the 13th century. It was a sign of quality – the 4 may have
represented upright scales and the XX a horizontal base.

Plate 5

The same symbol on a gravestone in the Howff, Dundee's medieval
burial ground, erected in 1763 for Thomas Smith, Merchant, and his
wife Barbara Hill.

TO THE

GUILDRY OF DUNDEE

GENTLEMEN,

You are requested to MEET within the GUILD HALL, on THURSDAY FIRST, the 9th day of March current, at Eleven o'clock forenoon, for the purpose of considering the proposed Dundee POLICE & IMPROVEMENT CONSOLIDATION BILL, and particularly the proposed interference with the rights, privileges & jurisdiction of the Guildry; and of resolving upon the action of the Guildry thereanent; and also for general business. I am,

GENTLEMEN,

Your most obedient Servant,

ALEX. HENDERSON,

DEAN OF GUILD.

DUNDEE, 6th March, 1882.

TO THE

Guildry of Dundee

GENTLEMEN,

You are requested to ASSEMBLE within the NEW CITY CHAMBERS, CRICHTON STREET, upon TUESDAY, the Twenty-Ninth October current, at Two o'clock afternoon, for the purpose of then and there putting in nomination Guild Brethren to be candidates for the office of DEAN OF GUILD for the year ensuing; as also for the purpose of electing ASSESSORS to the Dean, and the Clerk, Collector, and Officer, and for General Business.

You are further requested in case more than one Candidate shall be nominated at the Meeting of the Twenty-Ninth October current for the office of Dean of Guild, again to assemble within the New City Chambers, on Wednesday, the Thirtieth October current, at Eleven o'clock forenoon, for the purpose of electing by ballot, between the hours of Eleven forenoon and Two afternoon, one of the Guild Brethren put in nomination at the previous Meeting to be Dean of Guild for the ensuing year, all in terms of the Bye-Laws of the Guildry.

I am,

GENTLEMEN,

Your most obedient Servant,

SIMON FORREST,

DEAN OF GUILD.

Dundee, 21st October, 1929.

TO THE

GUILDRY OF DUNDEE

GENTLEMEN,

You are requested to MEET within the GUILD HALL on FRIDAY, the 6th November next, at Half-past Ten o'clock forenoon, for the purpose of Electing One Person to be a Director of the Corporation of the High School of Dundee for the year ensuing, under and in terms of the Provisions of the "William Harris Endowment "and Dundee Education Act, 1882."

I am, Gentlemen,

Your most obedient Servant,

DAVID DICKIE,

Dean of Guild.

Dundee, 27th October, 1914.

TO THE

GUILDRY OF DUNDEE

GENTLEMEN,

You are requested to MEET within the GUILD HALL, on Monday, the Seventh day of June next at Two o'clock Afternoon, for the purpose of electing FOUR GUILD BRETHREN—one of them being a Member of the Fraternity of Maltmen of Dundee— to be Directors of the Dundee Royal Lunatic Asylum on behalf of the Incorporation, for the year ensuing, in terms of the Charter of that Institution, and for General Business.

I am, Gentlemen,

Your most obedient Servant,

P. S. NICOLL,

Dean of Guild.

DUNDEE, 31st May, 1920.

Plate 6

Handbills for Guildry Members to attend meetings.
The practice of circulating these ceased in 1930, being replaced by newspaper intimations.

MEETING
OF THE
GUILDRY INCORPORATION.

WILLIAM THOMS, Esquire, Dean of Guild, Dundee.

DUNDEE, July 3, 1846.

SIR,

We request that you will convene the Guildry on an early day, to consider the propriety of voting an Address to Sir ROBERT PEEL, expressive of the sense of the Incorporation on those measures of Commercial Policy brought forward by him, and which have now received the sanction of Parliament; and also to consider the propriety of voting an Address to RICHARD COBDEN, Esquire, for his unwearied exertions in promoting the cause of Free Trade in Corn and other Provisions.

We are,

SIR,

Your most obedient servants,

Jas. Brown.	Alex. Balfour.	Will. Sime.	R. Gray.	G. M. Gray.
John Ewan.	Thomas Neish.	Andrew Guthrie.	Wm. Thomson.	P. Watson.
W. Geo. Baxter.	Peter Kinmond.	James McDonald.	James H. Bell.	John Sturrock.
Dad. Martin.	W. Johnston.	Jas. Lawson.	James Watt.	James Buchan.
Tho. Powrie.	Dad. Baxter.	Alexr. Steel.	James Fenwick.	Jno. Philp.
Arch. Crichton.	Alex. Kinmond.	J. T. Fairweather.	Wm. Murdoch.	And. Willison.
John Symers.	Geo. Thoms.	Edw. Baxter.	Wm. Paterson jr.	Wm. Wrongham.
James Wilson.	Alex. J. Warden.	Jas. Drummond.	James Paxton.	Wm. Halket jr.
Geo. Cochrane.	John Moir.	James Fleming.	John Mackay.	John Kennedy.
James Spankie.	Andw. Benvie.	P. Gardiner.	Alexr. Gilruth.	Wm. Nicoll.
James Webster.	Alex. Guthrie.	G. H. Nicoll.	Alex. Lawson.	John Fyffe.
D. Halley.	Chas. Norrie.	James Lennox.	Jas. Crawford.	Geo. N. Baxter.
John Bruce.	G. Jameson.	Robert Nicoll.	Thomas Garland.	Geo. R. Baxter.
James Pullar.	David Dick.	Peter Stuart.	Thos. Guthrie.	John Robertson.
Geo. Rough.	Wm. Maxwell.	John Tulloch.	David Tulloch.	Eben. Robertson.
Alexr. Hutcheson.	Alexr. Hamilton.	Henry Jack.	Thomas Simson.	John M. Banks.
Wm. Middleton.	James Fyfe.	Dav. Borrie.	Wm. Saunders.	William Scott.
Alex. Leask.	Thos. Russell.	W. Morris.	Wm. Jobson.	William Davidson.
John Hutcheson.	John Sinclair.	James Webster.	Wm. Ferrier.	Isac Low.
Geo. Oswr.	John Durham.	Peter Hean.	John Anderson.	Thomas Lamb.
John Watson.	D. Hutcheson.	Willm. Moyes.	P. H. Thoms.	John Lamb.
				Rob. Sturrock.

TO THE GUILDRY.

GENTLEMEN,

In compliance with the foregoing Requisition, I have to request that you will ASSEMBLE within the GUILD HALL, on MONDAY first, the 6th instant, at two o'clock afternoon, for the purposes stated in the Requisition. I am, Gentlemen, your most obedient servant,

WILLIAM THOMS, D.G.

DUNDEE, July 4, 1846.

Printed at the Advertiser Office, Dundee.

Plate 7

A rare notice from 1846 printed on silk – perhaps a presentation copy.

Plate 8

The Minute Book and accompanying leather case of the Dean of
Guild's Convivial Society, instituted in 1841. It last met just before
the Second World War but for the last 50 years the Lord Dean and
Assessors have met at country venues for convivial luncheons!

Plate 9

The Guildry were entrusted with regulating the Weights and
Measures of the Town. This picture shows seven weights from 56lb
downwards, inscribed "Anna Regina Auerdupois primo Maii
1707". They were made by J. Jamieson of Dundee.

Plate 10

The 1835 Imperial Bushel made by De Grave of London, and the
1826 Imperial Quart and Half Gallon also made by J. Jamieson.

Plate 11

Loaf-shaped Bakers' bronze weight for a Quartern (4lb) and Half Quartern (2lb), inscribed "Guildry of Dundee 1826".

Plate 12

An 18th century coopered dry measure for a mett. As recently as the mid 20th century, coal was still sold in Dundee by the mett or half mett.

Plate 13

The Kirkin of the Lord Dean in 1999 in Dundee Parish Church (St Mary's). The Lord Dean is seen with the Lord Provost; Guildry Clerk; Rector, Head Girl and Head Boy of the High School; Convenor of the Three United Trades; Assessors and Members of the Guildry.

Plate 14
Alexander Murdoch, elected Lord Dean in 2003, enrobed and
enchained. The gold chain, purchased for £65 in 1818,
is 21 feet long and weighs 12 ounces.

Plate 15

Stained glass window at the south end of the Huntingdon Aisle in
Dundee Parish Church, given by the Guildry to commemorate the
Octocentenary of the Church in 1990 and to celebrate the long and
close association between the Guildry and the Church.

Plate 16

Silver given by the Guildry: Candlesticks to the City to
commemmorate its Octocentenary in 1991; Salver to the City to
mark the Queen's Golden Jubilee in 2002; and Salver to Bernard C.
Bowman in 1991 to commemorate 20 years as Clerk. Following his
death it was re-presented to the Guildry by his family for the use of
each succeeding Lord Dean of Guild.

Plate 17

The Guild Hall at Tallinn, one of the towns in the Hanseatic League, where merchant guilds were very powerful and wealthy.

7

THE GUILDRY AND THE CHURCH

Guild brethren of course must have taken their place in Dundee life apart from their share in the activities of the Guildry. Not all of these are reflected in the incorporation's records but in the case of religious observance and any relationship with the church there is some evidence. The Guildry's privileges were granted officially by the town in return for services to the great church of St. Mary's in the Fields, where they financed a priest to say services at the altar of the Halie Bluid. The entry fee to the Guildry included money to provide wine for communion and wax for the candles. As the Guildry's surviving records date from after the Reformation, apart from the copy of the Merchants' Letter and the processes that followed it, we have no way of knowing exactly when or how this particular use of their finances ceased. We do know that Dundonians were early converts to the beliefs of the reformers. Their regular contacts with the countries on the continent of Europe where the Reformation began would have introduced them to the new teaching, and there can be no doubt of the sympathy and support these engendered in the town. One of the most eminent and active reformers, James Halyburton, remained a popular provost for over 30 years. William Christison, the first minister of the parish from 1560-1597, was also a prominent reformer, present at the first General Assembly of the new church, as were two elders, George Lovell and William Carmichael, bailies of the town, members of old Dundee families.

The church had been neglected for several years after the ravages on its structure during the English occupation of the 1540s, when it was used as stables, and Christison was a prime mover in forwarding its reconstruction. In 1561 a kirkmaster was appointed to take charge of the renovation of the choir to prepare it for Protestant worship. Those of the old chapels still existing were demolished and the vestments of the priests were sold by auction – to be altered to serve as gowns for the kirk to convert for Protestant worship what remained of the great medieval church.[1]

It is likely then that the Guildry's first direct material connection with the church ended about then, though in 1590 the dues collected from members and visiting merchants were still described as for the 'holy blood and ornaments thereof'.[2] However there is little said about these events in the Guildry's records and the first mention of religion in contemporary times appears in 1589. As the congregation grew there was need for a second church, and in 1588 the South Church, then called the Cross Church, had been founded over the south transept of the original St Mary's. This cost money of course and on 1 October 1582, the town council had ordered a collection to be made in the town kirk. The dean was to have a number of merchants elected to pass round the brod – the collecting plate – with the deacons of the Trades also helping. A contribution was compulsory and anyone who refused was to have some of his goods up seized to the amount collected the week before.[3]

A second minister, James Robertson, was serving the town, in what was called the second charge of St Mary's. The ministry was an active one and in August 1589 at a meeting in the council-house a complaint was received from the ministers of the burgh.[4] They declared they were finding a 'coldness and lack of former zeal' which was said to have been 'in the hearts of all persons' at the beginning of the changes in religious belief and practices. The court of the dean and his assessors immediately agreed that this zeal could not be 'reduced' to its former estate except by hearing it preached in the kirk, which could not be done without attendance there. Therefore they ordered that all members should 'repair to the hearing of godis word' in the kirk on the ordinary days appointed. Anyone found on the calsy – the causeway – or on the shore or who opened his booth doors on these ordinary days, Sunday and Friday, would be fined an increasing amount for each offence: 2s for the first time; 4s for the second; and then 5s for a further offence. It is not clear from the records whether the officer was excused from attendance to look for absentees or whether he would have to keep a register. But it is clear that he was to report such sinners and the collector was to be charged yearly with their fines in his accounts, which helped to ensure that all the fines were gathered in.

A few years later even stricter rules appeared, as the more Calvinist reformers became more powerful in the kirk. None was to be absent on Wednesday and Friday in time of sermon, nor were any booths to be open then. And it was not only the merchants who were to leave their booths at this time; their wives and servants were included in the prohibition. There was increasing emphasis on Sunday observance. This was not a purely Protestant move; in 1462, in Perth, it was decided that no staples should be sold on Sundays.[5] The Sabbath was to be 'keiped holie and not profaned be no gild brother'. A 10s fine was imposed on any shops that opened that day and a 40s fine would be laid on those 'sundrie gild brethren' who travelled 'furth of this burgh to Forfar, Kerremure, Brechin and uther places' where there were markets and buying and selling on the prohibited day, contrary to the commandments of God.

The sailing of ships on the Sabbath was also deplored, when merchants, mariners and other sailors profaned the holy Sabbath most slanderously by bearing burdens, drinking and other 'unlawful exercises'. Therefore no ship was to sail from Dundee on that day and a £10 fine was to be extracted from every merchant that sailed and from the master of each ship.[6] These rules may have been very effective initially but some had to be renewed in the next decade. Indeed, they had to be added to, for in 1607 the extra order was made that members were not to haunt taverns in the time of preaching or praying.[7] These fines added quite nicely to the Guildry's income. In 1613, William Blair, the farmer of fines for keeping booths open at the forbidden times, paid over £20.[8]

Controlling members' behaviour on Sundays was only one part of the Guildry's religious commitments. The new church had to be furnished to fit the services of the reformers. Seats had to be put in and the church did not provide these. They were built by individual members of the congregation or by bodies like the Guildry for use of their members – but at least initially, not for their wives and families – and they were the property of those who installed them. In 1600, the collector, Thomas Davidson, presented his accounts for 1598-99 and these revealed a deficit of £66 13s 4d. A memo below the statement notes that the deficit was found to be have been spent on 'bigging of new seats in the new Cross kirk' so his accounts were passed and Thomas was cleared of any debt to the Guildry.[9] In 1651 the occupying army, like its predecessors of the sixteenth century, used it to stable their horses. In the eighteenth century when another church was found necessary for the increasing population of the burgh, it was built on the site of the north transept which had been used as a graveyard. The sixteenth century church then became known as the South Kirk and the newer one took its name the Cross Kirk.

The Guildry had seats in the old kirk as well which must have been installed before we have their records. The Dunfermline Guildry in 1561 built enough seats in their parish church to accommodate all their members,[10] and it is likely that in devoutly Protestant Dundee the various societies did likewise. Initially these would be used by Guildry members only and were kept clean and in good condition by an officer appointed and paid by the Guildry. He not only looked after these seats but made sure at services that only Guildry brethren sat in them. It was the practice in presbyterian churches for members of the congregation to have their own appointed seats, for which they paid rents until these were abolished in the twentieth century. The Guildry paid regularly for 'keeping the seat': £8 in the East and £5 8s in the West kirk, and John Ramsay was at one point the officer who was paid £6 13s 4d at regular intervals for attending the church to regulate who sat there. He also repaired seats, on one occasion receiving £3 18s 6d for mending those in the old and new kirks.[11] The man who cleaned and repaired them did not receive just a salary; in the eighteenth century John Scott did not think his pay was sufficient and he asked for 'charity and cloathes' and he was duly provided with a new coat and a pair of shoes, which were renewed in 1728.[12]

The owners of seats were considered owners of the church and were expected to contribute to general repairs and alterations. They even provided their own lighting on some occasions for the 1799-

1800 accounts include 4d for 'candles to the passage when the Guildry left at the sacrament'. In 1837 considerable alterations were made to the South Church, for which all owners would have to pay. One of the changes was that a clock was proposed for the centre of the gallery where the seats belonged to the Guildry. This was agreed to – provided the tenants of the seats did not object. The Guildry, like other societies, had realised at some date that they could increase their income by renting out their seats which were not always required by their members. It would be surprising to find that none of the guild brethren joined one of the seceding religious groups who left the established Church of Scotland, though they remained mostly Protestant and presbyterian. No oath of religious conformity was required, so non-attendance at the town church services did not affect their membership. Seats left unused belonging to the Guildry were leased at public roups.[13]

The new church set up in Scotland in 1560 had a problem that was even more important than providing seats for the congregation. Much of the wealth of the Roman Catholic church needed to maintain its priests had lain in lands which had been transferred before the Reformation to laymen, most of whose families managed to retain control of the lands they had been awarded, usually by the monarch, and all the income pertaining to it. The new Protestant church was faced with having to provide for its ministry with little in the way of resources. It found the way by collecting stipends from the congregations for the sustentation of the ministry. By 1590 the Guildry had begun to pay their contribution of £47 from what had been originally collected to pay for their altar, and by 1660 they were paying £100 Scots. The town council was responsible for setting the amount paid, but the Guildry had to collect some of the stipend from other societies – and this could cause difficulties. In 1712 the Wigmakers and the Barbers had obtained an act of council about their members' freedom and they seemed to think that they were thereby relieved of paying some part of the £10 they were due towards the stipends. The dean complained to the head court about this and it was recommended that this should be considered again.[14] However the outcome was not recorded. The collectors sometimes got into debt over the stipends when they had not enough income to cover them but in 1717 they were refunded when the Guildry was repaid money owed for Newport harbour.[15] Another voluntary contribution to the church was also made by the Guildry. The catechists employed as assistants to the ministry, for example, were allowed 50 merks a year out of the Guildry's own funds.[16]

The payment of stipends became another source of discord between council and incorporation when the latter obtained control of their funds. When the town did return the Guildry's money to them there were discrepancies over the stipends which the dean and assessors noted. One of the few meetings recorded in the early part of the nineteenth century was summoned only because the council wished to increase the stipends. When the council finally disgorged the necessary papers it was discovered that the returns were inaccurate, but the Guildry did agree to pay all the council asked then.[17] Later, in 1850, the Guildry refused to help to increase the stipend of the minister of the South Church.[18] This quarrel was not settled until 1875 when the incorporation agreed to the £5 p.a. increase without the interest demanded by the council as hospital patrons, paying £70 to the hospital fund and £55 to the council to cover the amount that had accumulated.[19]

When the town awoke in January 1841 to find that a terrible fire had destroyed all their town churches but the Steeple Church and the old Steeple, the Guildry were immediately involved as proprietors in all the planning and financing of replacements. Incidentally, they also had to recompense the tenants of their seats in the two churches who had had to find another place of worship in the Lindsay Street church, for the seat rents they had to pay there.[20] At a general meeting on 4 August 1841 the sum of £5,206 was agreed by the owners for the rebuilding of the South Church, £5,618 16s for the East and £800 for removing the Cross Church.[21] On 19 May 1842, the Guildry were present with representatives of the Trades in the town and the Masonic Lodges when the foundation stone was laid for the new East or parish church, when a plate with an inscription was deposited in it. The Dundee Bank was paid £1 5s for their share of the expenses of the ceremony plus 4s to David Anderson for carrying the Guildry flag.[22]

There had been no doubts in the town that the East Church, the original parish church, should be rebuilt. A few months before this ceremony the dean had reported that he and others interested in rebuilding the South Church had met.[23] There was not universal approval for this despite the agreement on a price immediately after the fire. The actual expense had probably damped down the initial enthusiasm for rebuilding. Eventually in 1845 plans were agreed as long as the price was restricted to £3 3s per sitting. The Guildry agreed to bear their proportion as long as that was in fact the maximum. The first estimate of £4,685 10s worked out at £3 17s 6d per sitting, but Mr. Scott, the architect, agreed to modify the plans if this was possible without affecting the appearance or 'diminishing the stability' of the church and reduced the price by £300. However, the first price was agreed to and the rebuilding went ahead.[24] The payment of the Guildry's share was made in instalments of £67 in December 1845, April 1846 and December 1846, with a final payment of £58 2s 6d shortly thereafter. In November 1847, the South Church was almost finished and arrangements were made to let the Guildry's thirteen pews, though in May 1848 some were still available.[25]

The fire had given rise to a problem for another association in the town. The Coopers had written to the Guildry to explain that as their only property was their pews in the East Church they now had no funds to pay the stipends. The reply was that they either paid arrears or gave up the right of their seats to the Guildry.[26] This may seem harsh but all the proprietors of seats in the two churches were faced with the prospect of funding the new buildings and then providing the furnishings. The Guildry at a later time in fact claimed that the rents of their pews at £2 2s were very low when they were asked to pay a proportion of the cost of painting, cleaning and improving the East Church and they clearly grudged being asked for a contribution of £4 9s per seat.[27]

The incorporation began to feel the need for funds after the loss of their privileges in 1846. Membership declined for a time when it had few obvious benefits. In 1876 it was decided to end the free occupation of some of the Guildry pews in the South Church by the children of the Industrial School so that they could obtain rent. The council offered to buy their pews at £150 but the Guildry declared that £250 was the least they would accept and decided that the children would not be allowed in after the first Sabbath after the meeting. Thereafter they would have the pews cleaned and painted subsequent to letting them.[28]

During all these years there is no overt mention in the records of such dramas as the various secessions from the established Church of Scotland. Even the 1843 Disruption, which split the kirk in two and had such great effects on so many Scottish institutions, evoked no remark, except at a meeting of the Convivial Society in May 1843 (See Chapter 12). However, one incident may illustrate the views of some of the members on one of the main causes of dissension in the church before the Disruption – the question of who should appoint the minister to a congregation. The town council at that time were the patrons of the town churches and therefore were responsible for calling a minister to each of the charges. In 1826 there was a motion that the dean and the Guildry councillor should vote at the town council meeting for either James Thomson or David Davidson to fill a vacancy. An amendment reminded the meeting that the Guildry representatives on the council had to swear to vote for whom they thought best but that amendment was lost. The Guildry were not perhaps living up to their principles of belief in the independence of councillors by making a firm recommendation that the council should appoint David Davidson.[29] The discussion on this occasion may show some signs of the dislike of the power of patrons in appointments to the ministry which was one of the causes of the Disruption.

On another occasion, the guild brothers voted overwhelmingly for toleration in religion. A general meeting was summoned for 19 February 1829 to receive resolutions on the proposal for Roman Catholic emancipation. The state of Ireland was quoted as showing the evils arising from the existing position. An amendment that a petition should be prepared against emancipation, on the grounds that popery supported political tyranny, was defeated by a great majority. A petition was duly sent to Hugh Lindsay M.P. in favour of emancipation, which he promised would be presented the day after his letter acknowledging its receipt was written.[30]

The Guildry still maintain the connection with St Mary's which began in 1515. The incorporation installed a stained glass window in 1990. The minister there is their chaplain and each Lord Dean is 'kirked' at a special service in the church.[31]

NOTES

[1]   J.H. Baxter, *Dundee and the Reformation* (Dundee, 1960), 24-25.

[2]   DCA: G/1, 1590.

[3]   Maxwell, *History of Old Dundee*, 248.

[4]   DCA; G1/1, f.23 1-8-1589.

[5]   Stavert, *Perth*, iv.

[6]   DCA; G1/1, f.34, 16-10-1593.

[7]   DCA; G1/1, f.38, 10-2-1607.

[8]   DCA; G1/1, f.44, 1613.

[9]   DCA; G1/2, f.34, 3-1-1600.

[10] E.P.D. Torrie, *The Gild Court Book of Dunfermline* (S.R.S. New Series 12), 106.

[11] DCA; G1/1, f.91.

[12] DCA; G1/2, 18-6-1725, 1728.

[13] DCA; G1/5, 7-4-1820.

[14] DCA; G1/2, 27-6-1712.

[15] DCA; G1/2. 25-5-1717.

[16] DCA; G1/2, 17-2-1736.

[17] DCA; G1/4 , December 1817.

[18] DCA; G1/7, 25-12-1850.

[19] DCA; G1/8, 31-3-1875.

[20] DCA; G/6, 1 3-1-1841.

[21] DCA; G1/6, 4-8-1841.

[22] DCA; G1/7a, 28-5-1842.

[23] DCA; G1/7a , 30-3-1842.

[24] DCA; G1/7, 18-8-1845,12-9-1845.

[25] DCA; G1/7, 1-5- 1848.

26 DCA; G1/7a, 30-3-1842.
27 DCA; G1/8, 12-7- 1865.
28 DCA; G1/8, 29-3-1876, 26-4-1876.
29 DCA; G1/5, 8-5-1826.
30 DCA; G1/6, 6a., 19-2-1929, 13-5-1829.
31 Goodfellow, v.

8

RELATIONS WITH
THE DUNDEE TRADES

The merchants were not the only group in the burgh who found that common interest led them to form an association, but the Guildry was by far the most influential. Its regulation of trade and commerce was accepted; the majority of town councillors were merchants and the dean was a magistrate and councillor, while from 1642 another guild brother was also a member of the council. In many towns, from the fifteenth century at least, craftsmen too had been forming their societies to defend their position as skilled men and to maintain the standards of their crafts. Their incorporations were recognised legally by the town councils who granted *Seals of Cause*. In Dundee the Trades were pendicles of the Guildry, a status which meant that the latter had control over them in the last resort, but such authority was usually exercised with discretion. The craftsmen may have felt aggrieved sometimes by the Guildry's actions but over the centuries there seem to have been only few occasions in the burgh when relations between the groups threatened or roused real violence.

The first serious disagreement of which we have a record is the objections raised by the various crafts to the 1515 Merchants' Letter which gave the Guildry more powers over the Trades and more prestige in religious observance than the craftsmen thought reasonable. Once the need for arbitration had been accepted and arranged, the privileges of the two groups were legally defined as far as trade was concerned. The fact that craftsmen could become members of the Guildry if they wished, provided they ceased to practise their trade in person, must have helped to prevent some ill-feeling. Those craftsmen who did aspire to becoming guild brothers must have been the wealthiest and probably the most influential in their own trades. The Baker Trade tended to find itself at odds with the council which was responsible for fixing the prices of bread and ale. These could be altered depending on the value of grain and sometimes both bakers and brewers objected to this. In 1561 there was fear of dearth and the council tried to compel the bakers to take an oath to make loaves of a specific weight whatever the price of the grain. The bakers went to the Court of Session which relieved them of taking that oath but the incorporation's fight was with the town council, not the Guildry specifically.[1] Indeed, as we have seen, in the nineteenth century the Guildry expressed doubts as to whether it had any power where bread was concerned.

From the middle of the sixteenth century, however, craftsmen began to show signs of wanting more influence in the country and in Dundee they persisted in attempts to win a greater part in the administration of the burgh. In 1563, a meeting of parliament had been called. The commissions to the burgh's two representatives, appointed by the council, had to be legally validated by having the common seal of the burgh attached to them. Alexander Carnegy, collector of the crafts, was keeper of one of the three keys that were necessary to open the common kist in which the seal was kept, and he refused to cooperate. He declared that he had been forbidden to do so by the deacons of the crafts as both commissioners were merchants and the Dundee craftsman wanted one of their members to be appointed.[2] As there was no roll of those present at that parliament, it is not known whether the two originally appointed were allowed to sit, with or without the seal to give authenticity to their commissions. The episode is important in illustrating both the growth of craft confidence and undoubtedly some resentment at the dominance of the merchant class.

A much more serious quarrel involving council, Guildry and Trades erupted at the beginning of the seventeenth century. Apart from the provost and magistrates the council at that time consisted of nine merchant councillors and two craftsmen. Led by two prominent men in the town, one a bailie, Robert Flesher, and the other the minister of the first charge, Robert Howie, the craftsmen demanded that they should have two more representatives on the council.

Howie has been described as being of 'a hott and vehement humour'[3] and rioting began in December 1603, when the crowd refused to obey the magistrates' order to go quietly home. Howie at this point declared that the council were all 'partial' and he would admit to no judges but the deacons of the crafts. Things went from bad to worse with Howie inciting the populace to violence. An appeal was made to the Convention of Royal Burghs which was meeting in Perth in September 1604. Despite Howie's appearance outside that town with several hundred armed men the craftsmen lost their case. Then the opposition, including members of the current council, elected their own council, choosing Thomas Man as dean of the Guildry. Over the next couple of years there was some jockeying for power, though the substitute council elected by Howie's supporters seems to have left no records. The legal council did eventually agree to having three craftsmen elected, with the proviso that if no proof of having the right to four was shown the number would revert to two.

The Privy Council was involved and talked of Flesher as one of those 'ambitiously aspyring' to the government of the burgh and having made Dundee, which they declared was 'in all aiges bigane (bygone) ane haill bodie of quiet modest and honest citizens', now a 'town of war'. The election of the second council was declared unlawful and Thomas Man was to be imprisoned in Blackness Castle.[4] Howie was banished to St Andrews and eventually deprived of his charge. Plague appeared from 1606 onwards and tended to make health a more pressing problem than election of town councillors but the discontent did not immediately evaporate.

This discord is sometimes represented as a typical example of the rivalry between crafts and guilds but there is another element in this row which should be considered. The provost from 1601 was Sir James Scrymgeour, a favourite of James VI, and also Constable of Dundee. Scrymgeour was a formidable figure and it would seem that the councillors were as much his henchmen as their successors in the time of Alexander Riddoch were his. It has been suggested that the council accepted the king's nominee to assist them in opposing the growth of the influence of the Trades which was encouraging expression of the voice of the people of the town.[5] Similar tendencies can be seen within the Guildry when the voicing of too many opinions was regarded as causing confusion in their decisions. Apart from that aspect, the constable was never popular with the townspeople, partly because as Constable he had tried, even when not on the council, to exert more power in the town than the inhabitants liked. It is possible that some of the unrest was directed not so much at the Guildry as at him and the riots in 1604 began with stones being thrown at his house.[6] At least, after he lost his position in the 1609 elections, while the craftsmen were not perhaps wholly satisfied, they made no great objections to an extra merchant councillor when they were assured this was not threat to their liberties. Both council and deacons bound themselves to 'keep skaithless' (unharmed) the present provost and bailies and peace returned to the town.

Fortunately perhaps for the peace of the town, the Guildry's interest in the trade incorporations tended to be erratic. The Trades, especially those which formed their own union of the Nine Trades, seem always to have been strong enough and confident of their privileges, once they had their *Seals of Cause*, to stand up for themselves, as was seen in 1515. There does not seem to have been any suggestion that they needed the Guildry's approval to elect a convener or work together. The Wrights, Masons and Slaters, later than the Nine in obtaining their *Seals of Cause*, did ask permission to join together to form the United Trades in 1741, primarily because they wished to buy meal in bulk, thereby gaining better terms for their members.[7]

Earlier in the eighteenth century, the Wrights were at odds with the Guildry over the management of their funds and there was also difficulty over the employment of an unfree wright by a merchant. In 1711 the Guildry ordered that the payment of some debt owed by the Trade must not be made out of the Wrights' poor fund. It is not clear who the creditor was, but their visitor had ignored this command.[8] Some years later the dean had been informed that the Wrights had used their poor fund to apply to a private debt and the Wrights were to be summoned to have their accounts inspected and to answer this charge.[9] Later that year, the Wrights made what was potentially a much more serious complaint against George Ramsay, a merchant and guild brother, and a former provost. They accused him of employing Henry Duncan, an unfree wright, that is one who was not a member of their incorporation, newly come into the town to live, to glaze Ramsay's new lodging in the Overgate. They pointed out the 'great hurt and prejudice' this caused to members of their Trade who as burgesses 'had to pay cess, i.e. taxation, stipends, to quarter soldiers, and to the burden of watch and ward, part of all public burdens'. Claiming the sole right of their Trade to the monopoly of all wright work, they referred to fines imposed by the Guild court and the magistrates on any who breached this monopoly.

Ramsay's defence was interesting. He contended that any guild brother was entitled to employ an unfree man, as the Wright Trade was 'only a pendicle of the Guildry'. Fortunately for the good relations between Guildry and Trade, a committee of the former ordered the Guildry officer to stop Duncan working as either wright or glazier in the burgh. At the time Ramsay protested and demanded that the Wright Trade produce proof of their claims, but the vote went in favour of the Trade. Two days later, however, Ramsay produced a receipt for Duncan's burgess ticket. As a result the Wrights' demand for a fine was passed to the dean, the magistrates and the guild councillor. Their decision does not seem to have been reported in the Guildry's records but the sudden appearance of this receipt does raise a question – had Ramsay hastily paid the burgess fee for his employee when the decision of the Guildry went against him? The date of the receipt was not mentioned in the minutes.[10]

There was acrimony between the Wrights particularly and other trades and the Guildry on several occasions about the use of mortcloths. In 1753 the dean was instructed to recommend that the Wrights should not rent their mortcloths to any but their own members and certainly should not encroach on the Guildry's privileges by giving them to any guild brother.[11] In 1818, and at other times in the nineteenth century, incorporations were accused of letting their mortcloths to guild members with consequent loss of income to the Guildry.[12] As we have seen the Guildry's were more expensive.

In 1723 there was some general discussion about the status of various trades. The dean pointed out that the Masons and Coopers, though pendicles of the Guildry, who contributed £6 and £5 respectively through the Guildry towards the ministers' stipends, did not seem to want any share in the privileges of the guild brethren. The town council had suggested that the Wigmakers and Barbers should be incorporated as a pendicle. The dean's court disapproved of the idea so they may never in fact have become a formal society,[13] but in 1783 nineteen barbers were mentioned as comprising a pendicle trade. The Cooper Trade – the barrelmakers – numbered fourteen, but the Dundee Register from which these numbers come included six shipbuilders, hat and last makers as members of that Trade.[14] Apothecaries and surgeons sometimes cast longing eyes on becoming part of the Guildry but they got no encouragement and, as has been noted earlier, were warned that paying apprentice fees did not give them access to the Guildry's privileges.

The Maltmen's relationship with the Guildry was altogether more ambiguous. For a start, in 1567 parliament had laid down that maltmen could neither have a deacon nor ever be considered a craft. In 1669 the second parliament of Charles II ratified this act and added that any office such as deacon, visitor, boxmaster, or any other claiming similar powers among maltmen should cease in all burghs. The town council of Edinburgh, which had ranked Maltmen among their many trades, was ordered to erase the name from their register. Furthermore, no burgh was to presume in future ever to grant these tradesmen such a privilege. If maltmen did meet as such, they would be fined 500 merks, half going to the informer of the occasion, in addition to any punishment of the offenders by the Lords of the Privy Council.[15] However, the Maltmen in Dundee opened a Locked Book in 1623 and are categorised in 1872 as a pendicle though at that point they had only three members, a sharp drop from the fifty listed in 1783.[16] Also, despite the 1669 ratification of the 1567 legislation, at a meeting of the Royal Burghs at Perth in 1673, 'incorporations' of maltmen are mentioned when gifts made by the king which affected their rights were discussed. These gifts might possibly include the right to brew or to tax ale. The burgh of Edinburgh was asked to assist them in opposing any new gifts which might damage the 'said incorporations'.

Whatever their corporate circumstances, at the end of the seventeenth and the beginning of the eighteenth century, Dundee town council's financial difficulties effected a change in the Dundee Maltmen's position. After the travail of the burgh in 1651, the Maltmen had taken on themselves to pay one merk per boll of malt steeped to help the town, a tax which the council had continued in 1669. Each maltman had also paid £4 Scots to the Guildry for the liberty to carry on their trade in the burgh and each apprentice £2 Scots as his indenture fee. However, such payments conferred no privileges of the Guildry on these tradesmen. They were managed separately, and could not hold any office in Dundee or become members of the Guildry or the Nine Trades. In 1690, however, the town made another appeal for financial help to which the maltmen responded conditionally. One of these was that the political disabilities laid on them should be removed, so that they could form their own society, appointing the usual officials, and join others.

Another demand was that the fee of 40 merks paid to the Guildry for the privilege of being allowed to 'upset their booths' should not be increased; this could be guaranteed by the council's control of the Guildry. For eleven years they would pay 10s on each boll of meal to the hospital fund. Nothing was said about maltmen paying £4 for their freedom though it was expressly stipulated that apprentices should pay as before. It would appear that thereafter maltmen entered the Guildry free if they wished to, and records appear to confirm this, as three were entered free in 1701 and others on later dates, paying only the price of setting up their shops or booths, without being charged for the other usual 'accidents'. In 1713 the collector booked a maltman as freemaster of that trade, however, not of the Guildry. It seems clear from the records that maltmen were not bound to enter the Guildry unless they chose. If they did, they thereafter paid the same dues as merchants, while by paying only £4 Scots to the Guildry they could still carry on their trade as brewers, selling their own beer and ale in their own booths. Few chose the more expensive option.[17]

From this time it seems that they were also to pay 10d Scots on each steeping of malt and as a 'branch' of the Guildry they were to contribute £50 Scots towards the ministers' stipends.[18] The council had also granted the Maltmen the concession of being allowed to elect a deacon or visitor and also a collector of these sums. This was a flagrant breach of the laws of Scotland. In 1701 the council, still in financial straits, saw an opportunity of obtaining more income from one of their most important assets, the town mills. A committee of the council and the Guildry met with a group of maltmen to try to increase the rents paid by the brewers. The Maltmen offered 9,000 merks (£6,000 Scots) yearly while the town asked for 12,000 (£8,000 Scots), and within a few months a compromise was reached: 7,000 merks (£4,666 Scots) was to be paid yearly for five years and during that time brewers were to be freed of paying cess – a tax regularly laid on inhabitants. Acts in favour of brewers were to be renewed.[19]

The Guildry complained in 1707 that the Maltmen who 'are a branch of the Gildrie' were refusing to pay their contribution to the stipends for the parish ministers. On 17 September of that year, the Guildry presented a petition to the magistrates and town council, pointing out that they feared that the magistrates would be unable to recover any dues which contributed towards paying the stipends. They reminded the council of the acts passed by the Scottish parliament and asked that the council acts contrary to these should be annulled. Thereby the appointment of a deacon or boxmaster of Maltmen would once again be forbidden in Dundee. In their place it was suggested that the dean of the Guildry should be allowed to collect all these dues. The provost, bailies and council agreed to all this. They could hardly refuse, as their authorising maltmen to elect a deacon and boxmaster was illegal. Thereafter the Guildry collector was to uplift the dues on each steeping of malt and the maltmen apprentices were to pay 40s at entry, which the collector would record in his accounts. In the 1707-8 Guildry accounts £23 7s 8d was paid to the collector from the 10d imposition on malt steeping and, in 1709-10, booked maltmen were entered separately.[20]

From this time onwards, the Maltmen, though having been described as part of the Guildry, exercised somewhat precarious independence. They had their own officer, but in 1712 had no funds to pay for him, so the Guildry bailed them out for the future 'during the Guildry's pleasure'.[21] Later that year a joint committee was appointed with three guild brothers sitting on it. In 1723 the Guildry chose the maltman who would keep the Maltmen's mortcloth and a committee of Guildry was to audit his accounts.[22] With their entry fees going to the Guildry, the Maltmen were not in a strong financial position. They still collected for their poor but out of their 'private pockets'. In September 1723 they had once again to petition the Guildry for help 'being under the Gildrie', as their poor were so numerous that they were incapable of providing for them. The Guildry decreed that in future every apprentice maltman should pay £4 Scots – £2 for the use of the Guildry and £2 for the poor. A master's fee would be £8 similarly divided, and a stranger setting up as maltman would be due £12, all paid to the Guildry collector while a maltman, chosen by the Maltmen but with the Dean of Guild present, would be in charge of their poor fund.[23] Maltmen were also to become burgesses.

They could still collect for their separate poor fund 10d from all the malt they steeped for their own use and also the 6s 8d from that made for the use of 'noblemen, gentlemen or strangers', out of which they should give to the Guildry the £50 Scots per annum towards the Dundee ministers' stipends. This contribution was paid until 1846 when the Maltmen refused to pay their dues, in lieu of the 10d on each steeping of malt, but this was not accepted by the Guildry.[24] After several meetings at which no agreement could be reached, the Guildry took steps to begin a case in the sheriff court to recover what they considered due debts.[25] The Maltmen's funds would not allow them to fight any such legal action and they had already resolved that, without admitting liability, they would offer their seats in the church in full and final discharge of the debt.[26] In 1852 they gave up their three pews and three seats in the Old or East parish church, thereby being relieved of paying part of the stipend – formerly £50 Scots, or £4 3s 4d sterling.[27] The Maltmen lost any income they made if they had been renting their church seats to members of the congregation, but by ridding themselves of the seats they also shed any liability for repairing or rebuilding the church. It was agreed that the expenses of conveyancing and any discharge required by the Maltmen was to be at mutual expense but if an assignation of the tax on each steeping of barley was required the Maltmen were to pay the expenses of that. The rent of the seats was £100 but the value of the debts due, the duty on malt at £70 and the other costs involved, came to £100 17s 3d, with payment of the difference to be arranged.[28]

It is hardly surprising that the Maltmen were not completely satisfied with the situation in which they found themselves after 1707, especially as the price of their main product, ale, which was the common drink of the day, was wholly outwith their control. By 1739 they seem to have taken upon themselves to appoint a visitor, a less powerful leader than a deacon, and in that year the Guildry received a request for redress for their grievances from James Blair the holder of that post.[29] This seems to have been ignored and the following year the Maltmen attempted to take action. They formed an association among themselves to make arrangements about the selling of ale, drew up a contract upon stamped paper and signed it. As this was still an illegal proceeding, Robert Stirling, who had custody of the document, was summoned to appear before the Dean of Guild's Court with it. It was duly read out and delivered to the dean to be disposed of as he thought fit.[30] The maltmen seem to have persevered in their intention to form their own society and their own first sederunt book opens in 1786. They must already have had some sort of unofficial organisation as their register of apprentices opens in 1653.[31]

For some years after the drastic destruction of the contract in 1740, the Guildry records do not specifically include any discussion on the position of the Maltmen, though there was always one maltman among the four directors elected from guild brethren to sit on the board of the lunatic asylum, and as trustees on the Harbour Trust set up in the nineteenth century. A rather ridiculous situation arose over the election of the maltman director to the board of the lunatic asylum in 1822. The Maltmen stood on their dignity, met in the Old Kirk and elected their deacon, Andrew Hood. The Guildry reacted by examining the constitution of the asylum, found that it was their duty to elect four directors, 'one of whom must be a maltman' – and promptly elected Andrew Hood![32]

The question of the Maltmen's relationship with and their entry to the Guildry arose officially once more from 1815 onwards. From a letter written by the Guildry clerk, it would seem that the Maltmen had certainly not forgotten their claims nor neglected opportunities to put them forward at least semi-officially. As they paid dues for free apprentices and £4 4s to the Guildry and 5s to the hospital fund, as well as 13s 4d to the officer, they thought they had some right to its privileges and they formed a committee of seven in March 1815 to investigate what they termed their 'ancient rights'.[33] In 1815 too, they had refused to join the procession to lay the foundation stone of the harbour unless they were officially included among the Guildry. This was conceded and they were informed that they must wear black, the Guildry 'uniform'. New bye-laws had been drawn up regarding entry to the Guildry at the close of the fight with the council and in March a copy of the agreement between the town of Dundee and the Maltmen regarding entry fees was presented to the Guildry. This was sent to Mr. James Ivory, their legal adviser, for an opinion but he was somewhat dilatory in considering it and there was a suggestion that if the Maltmen's claim for cheaper or free entry was not sustained, it would be reasonable to allow them three months on the more favourable terms.[34]

In June 1818 the clerk of the Guildry, James Saunders, wrote to Robert Whitton, described as deacon of the Maltmen, pointing out that it had always been his opinion that, as the Maltmen were so sure that they had a right to entry to the Guildry on more modest terms than the merchants, they should employ a clerk, by which he meant a legally qualified official, to prepare a statement of the basis of their claim.[35] He went on to say that the Maltmen expected that he would do this for them as they had contributed generously to the Guildry's process against the magistrates and he then went on to do just that. He argued that all the town council did was to remove the political 'incapabilities' of the Maltmen in return for financial aid and as we have seen this favour was revoked in 1707. In September the brewers were asked to send a memorial without delay giving their grounds for claiming lower entry fees. The Maltmen themselves had a long memo on counsel's opinion on their claim which was to be inserted in their sederunt book, but unfortunately this did not happen.[36] There were two meetings of the Guildry in November, at the first of which the memo was read and a motion in favour of acceptance of the Maltmen's claim was proposed. At the second the proposer, Mr. Thornton, withdrew his earlier motion but instead proposed that the 'Maltmen fraternity' should be allowed entry for £10 for three months and then pay ordinary dues. This was agreed to.[37] The Maltmen's generous contribution of thirty guineas to the Guildry's legal costs in its fight with the town council may well have assisted their case.[38]

In November 1820 the Maltmen were entered in a body, the Guildry clerk complaining bitterly of inadequate remuneration for all the work involved.[39] Whether this was justified is doubtful. In 1828 the oldest member of the Maltmen, George Corton, wrote to his Trade, regarding the unfairness of the tax on ale, claiming that little imported ale or porter was taxed but significantly he added 'our number here is so small as we are not an incorporated body.'[40] By 1872, there were apparently only three members of the association, though the society is rather larger now.

As far as relations with the other trades in the town were concerned, there is little in the earlier records of much contact except where individual craftsmen were suspected of 'encroachments'. One such occasion arose when William Hog, deacon of the Bonnetmakers incorporation, was accused by the collector, John Ramsay, of buying and selling rock indigo and wool in the burgh without having the freedom of the Guildry. Deacon Hog denied firmly that he sold these raw materials – the basic ingredients in the making of bonnets. He claimed that he gave them to members of his trade and then bought the bonnets made after paying for the making of them. The collector retorted that he could prove that Hog made a profit in this transaction and that this was plain merchandising. Also he had bought twenty pounds weight of indigo from an unfree mariner – such dealings between a freeman and an unfreeman being of course illegal. As Hog refused to testify or give his oath he was held to have in effect confessed and was duly fined £40 Scots though the dean was allowed to modify the fine as he thought fit. Hog was also forbidden to carry on such trading in future unless he became a member of the Guildry.[41]

There was change towards closer and more amiable contacts during the Guildry's struggle with the town council. Then the Nine Trades supported them whole-heartedly and the Guildry appreciated the presence of the convener at council meetings as well as financial help. Like the Maltmen they seem to have contributed thirty guineas towards the Guildry's legal expenses. By then many craftsmen were also guild brethren, having agreed not to exercise their trade personally, but only by employing servants. One restriction was placed on all who were members of both a Trade and the Guildry. They could exercise their voting rights in only one capacity and they had to declare which they chose. The good feeling engendered by the events of the second decade of the century did not evaporate and the loss of all privileges in 1846 made questions of control academic. Today many men are members of both groups which are now more social than professional gatherings.

NOTES

[1]   Maxwell, *History of Old Dundee*, 94.

[2]   Maxwell, *History of Old Dundee*, 185.

[3]   Flett, 'Conflict', 152.

[4]   RPC, vii, 736, 737.

[5]   Flett, 'Conflict', 148.

[6]   Flett 'Conflict' 153.

[7]   DCA; G1/2; Smith, *United Trades*, 30.

[8]   DCA; G1/2,2a, 26-8-1711.

[9]   DCA; G1/2, 1-7-1728, 6-7-1728.

[10] DCA; G1/2, 16-11-1728, 18-11-1728.

[11] DCA; TC56/2, 7-5-1753.

[12] DCA; G1/4, 19-3-1818.

[13] DCA; G1/2, 2-2-1723.

[14] Warden, 572.

[15] *APS*, iii, 33, c.37; *APS*, vii, 574; G8/104.

[16] Warden, 572, 605.

[17] DCA; HF/M/3/2, 10.6.1818; DCL; Lamb 195(9).

[18] DCA; G4/1, 10-6-1818, Letter from James Saunders to Robert Whitton, deacon of the Maltmen.

[19] DCA; G1/2, 26-11-1701, 19-3-1702.

[20] DCA; G3/1.

[21] DCA; G1/2, 7-10-1712.

[22] DCA; G1/2, 2-1-1723.

[23] DCA; G1/2, 21-9-1723.

[24] DCA; G1/7, 30-12-1846.

[25] DCA; G1/7, 29-8-1850, 22-10-1851.

[26] DCA; G1/7, 18-12-1851.

[27] I have to thank Gavin Cowper for showing me this uncatalogued discharge by the maltmen which he found among the records of the Dean of Guild Court in 1999.

[28] DCA; G1/7, 7-1-1851.

[29] DCA; G1/2, 28-2-1739.

[30] DCA; G1/2, 12-5-1740.

[31] DCA; HF/M/1/1, 2/1.

[32] DCA; G1/5, 22-4-1822.

[33] DCA; HF/M/1, 7-3-1815.

[34] DCA; G1/4, 19, 27, 30-3-1818.

[35] DCA; G4/1, June 1818.

[36] DCA; HF/M/1/1, 29-8-1818.

[37] DCA; G1/5, November 1818.

[38] DCA; HF/M/1/1, 6-4-1816.

[39] DCA;G1/5, 13-11-1820.

[40] DCA; HF/M /3/2 Bundle 5.

[41] DCA; G1/2, 29-12-1716.

9

THE NEWPORT FERRY

Probably the greatest, certainly the most expensive venture of the Guildry was one which could not really have been described as defending their privileges, except that if it had been successful it would have certainly benefited their funds greatly. It involved them in great outlay of time and money and was a heavy responsibility for about half a century. This was the development of the facilities of the ferry to Dundee from the south side of the Tay at the Seamills which became known as Newport – initially Newport of Dundee. This project was embarked on solely on the recommendation of the council whose finances at the time could not have stood the expense needed. There were several ferries across the Tay and the Woodhaven ferry was used more regularly before the eighteenth century than the ferry at Newport. The latter was used mostly for the carriage of grain for the mills of Dundee, which the Dundee council bought to supply the burgh's growing population.

In April 1713 it was reported to the Guildry court that the council was perturbed by the lack of use of that passage. It was thought that one reason for this might be the lack of suitable accommodation for strangers on the Fife side. There was only one house there and the town council suggested that it might benefit both town and Guildry if the latter 'bestowed part of their stock' in buying land 'about the sea mylns'. A tenant could be provided with a good house which could also be an inn for travellers, as well as offices and all that was necessary to improve the passage.[1] The dean and his court approved of this unanimously and within three days reported that the place in Fife had been inspected and found very suitable for a harbour. Their immediate adoption of this scheme is a little surprising for two years before they had been refused, initially at least, to consider being taxed to install buoys on the Tay. This proposal of the Fraternity of

Seamen had been discussed in February, 1711, but by September there must have been a change of heart. It emerged that the lighthouses were also in a bad state. That was not good for trade, and it was agreed then that buoys should be provided but that there should be more lights, and that they should petition parliament to have buoys paid for in the same way as the lights, by a tax imposed by an act.[2]

By 4 May 1713, three and a half acres had been bought from the estate of 'Enverdovat', (Inverdovat, now Tayfield) at the cost of £924 Scots, payable at Martinmas or as soon after as the Guildry was provided with a proper disposition of the land free of encumbrances.

It was in fact June 1736 before all the legalities referring to the title of the land were completed. The town's agent, James Preston, for some reason advised that the owners should dispone the lands to some trustee for the Guildry who would obtain the charter and assign precept of sasine to the incorporation. George Dempster, the prominent businessman and landowner, was chosen to be trustee in February 1736. Despite the lack of documentary proof of ownership, the Guildry had decided in 1713 to build three houses and a pier immediately.

On 20 May 1713, a committee of eleven which included several guild brethren who had also been bailies of the town was appointed to deal with 'everything relating to the project' – house-building and furnishing, making necessary highways and finding approved tenants. By August, Guildry funds were beginning to show signs of strain. On the eighth of that month the dean was instructed to write to all deans of guild to the north of Dundee as well as to provosts and magistrates, to ask for contributions, on the grounds that improvements to this important ferry would be of benefit not just to Fife and Dundee. At the same time the Justices of the Peace in Cupar were asked for assistance in repairing the high road from Newport to Kirkcaldy. The second appeal was more successful than the first. With the labour of two men allowed from each ploughland adjacent to the road with 3s per day each of bread and ale, by 9 September most of the road was made good, except for one part which had to wait until the corn was off the ground. There were no replies from the burghs to the north. However, the council had repaid one bond of £100 sterling owed to the Guildry and the interest on another, which had been resting since 1711 and these sums had paid for part of the cost of the land and houses.[3]

At the end of October when accounts were called for, satisfaction was expressed as far as the efforts of the merchant, James Greig, responsible for house furnishing and building the pier, were concerned. This was perhaps an over-optimistic view for contributions were to be called for towards the cost of the pier were the following month Henry Ramsay, a professor of philosophy at St Andrews University, as cautioner for George Coupar, who was to manage the new ferry, complained that the house would not be habitable for months. He wanted a 6% reduction in the rent until the following Whitsunday for house and harbour, though he was happy to pay for the attached land. His request was refused and Ramsay was still paying the tack duty in 1717, though he had asked to be relieved of it the year before. The Guildry had agreed if he would provide a suitable tenant.[4] Later, in 1730 it emerged that Ramsay had paid three years' rent to Whitsunday 1716, while Coupar was 'out of the way'. There were no accounts of Coupar having spent anything on the ferry but Ramsay was claiming over £400. A committee set to investigate this found that Ramsay had some genuine claim and offered him £200 which he accepted.[5]

A public roup was decided on in 1716 at which George Ramsay was authorised to offer 400 merks Scots[6] yearly on behalf of the Guildry. His offer won the roup and in August, a Kinghorn man, Robert Aiken, offered £20 sterling for six to nine years. He offered to pay 400 merks for the buildings and a malt barn if he remained there for the last three years of his tack, to repair the malt kiln as well as providing carriage for the necessary materials for repairs to the harbour, to slate the house and leave everything in good condition.

Finance was a problem from the outset. In April 1714, £162 11s 0d was collected from the town's inhabitants for defraying the cost of the 'harbour on the south side',[7] and in January 1714 the dean had suggested that at a meeting of the Convention of Royal Burghs, a collection should be requested from as far north as Inverness towards it. This was not an outrageous idea; the burghs often helped each other out when harbours or bridges, for instance, needed repair. In October of that year the dean reported that he must borrow £10 sterling to pay the workmen, something that could not be delayed. By March 1715, costs had risen to £4,640 13s 2d Scots, of which £1,159 18s 10d was still unpaid. A further blow in July 1716 was the collapse of part of the pier. The architect employed to inspect it had bad news. He reckoned the pier had too narrow foundations and was not properly built. He estimated that no less than £450 Scots was needed to repair and improve it. Initially this offer was accepted but in October the dean and his assessors pointed out that such expenditure was out of the question. After what was described as 'mature deliberation', the unfortunate dean was recommended to employ workmen as he saw fit and to build up the 'slop' of the pier in the best way that could be done at that time. It must have been small consolation to him that a committee of old bailies was to advise him, if required. Two Dundee masons were employed at a cost of 500 merks with the Guildry furnishing the materials, the last 200 merks to be paid at the completion of the repairs.[8]

It is not surprising to find that in August 1717 the proposal by an anonymous person to buy the Guildry's interest in Newport was at first favourably received. In February 1718, however, there was a change of heart and the offer of 8,000 merks by a vintner, a Mr. Gentleman, was refused despite the fact that there was apparently a further collapse of a part of the pier, though this reference may merely show that repairs were not yet complete: the records are not clear.

In the following years, this decision may have been regretted. There were continual problems with tenants who gave up their tacks prematurely or failed altogether to pay rent. This happened so often that the conclusion might be drawn either that the ferry was not really a very profitable proposition or that the Guildry were poor judges of tenants; the history of the ferry indicates that both these premises are correct. On several occasions when the tack was once again rouped, a representative of the Guildry was authorised to offer a low rent on its behalf, in the hope that a tenant might be found who would pay slightly more. In July 1728, Thomas Gentleman, who may be the same man who offered to buy the whole ferry ten years before, offered £8 sterling for three years and £28 10s, the current rent, for another four. By March 1731 he was having difficulty in paying any rent but he was allowed to continue his tenancy at a reduced amount, the Guildry maintaining the harbour and stock houses, the tenant the thatched houses. Even with such concessions, Gentleman still failed to pay any rent and he was compelled in September 1733 to sell his corn, cattle and his share of any of the ferry boats to cover his arrears. After he died, some time between then and April 1734, even a copper cauldron lying in the weighhouse was given to the Guildry as part of his arrears.

Yet another vintner, Alexander Aitkin, took on the tack in 1747 at £18 5s sterling.[9] He carried out unauthorised repairs and despite attempts to evict him through court actions and roups when other offers were accepted, he was still in possession in 1756. He had had earlier dealings with the Guildry when he asked for the repayment of at least part of £100 Scots he had paid for his freedom. He had declared that because of the decay of trade he had no intention of returning to Dundee and he was given the money on condition that he gave up all claims on the Guildry, so it is a little surprising that they considered him at all as a tenant.[10] His obstinacy involved the Guildry in other financial difficulties. Would-be tenants claimed damages for expenses they had incurred when Aitkin refused to move,[11] and one collector, George Hallyburton, had foolishly taken credit in his annual 'compt' for rent Aitkin had not paid. However, the auditors found that Hallyburton had also included other moneys he had not received so incompetent accounting may also have added to the Guildry's troubles at this time.[12]

Apart from unsatisfactory tenants, more of the Guildry's funds were absorbed by the ferry than it ever earned. Repairs and rebuilding were a continual expense, to the harbour, the offices, and the lodgings built for passengers who needed accommodation when the weather was too bad for a crossing or when no boat was available. A new kiln had to be built in 1725. So worrying was the financial situation that a committee appointed to visit all the offices and houses in Newport in the autumn in 1727 refused to go over unless they were given detailed instructions as to what they were expected to do. They were only moderately satisfied with a new stair for the harbour, a brewhouse, a henhouse and two large stables. An old boatman's house was ruinous and two new ones needed clay chimneys though 'otherwise sufficient'. The town council helped a little in 1736 by repaying a debt of £800 but other factors worked against the Guildry. Vessels went into Newport harbour and unloaded coal and other goods without paying tonnage or shore dues, thus avoiding Dundee dues as well. In March 1729, an attempt was made to correct this and the tenant was made responsible for collecting the same dues as were charged in Dundee.[13]

All the ferry lands were put up for sale in October 1749, as rents had been poorly paid for several years and the subjects were declared to be a 'burden on the Gildrie's stock'.[14] There was no sale then but in the 1757-58 accounts the Newport rent has disappeared. David Maxwell of Bogmiln had offered to buy all the property and paid a first instalment of £310 towards it. The remainder never materialised and each year the accounts include £180 still due with the interest on that sum added annually.[15] As a result the Guildry's connection with the ferry continued until the 1780s, by which time Maxwell had become bankrupt and the trustees for his creditors sold the former Guildry lands in Newport in March 1782. An Edinburgh lawyer offered £340 on behalf of the current owners of the estates of St Fort and Inverdovat so that they could regain the few acres sold to the Guildry when they began to develop the ferry. With interest the price offered grew to £358 11s 10d[16] but Maxwell still owed £21 14s 9d, for which the Guildry accepted 10s in the pound amounting to £15 15s.[17]

The society must have been glad to be relieved of what had become such a burden to them though no doubt of some benefit to travellers. And Dundee town council too must have been delighted that they had persuaded another body to accept responsibility for what should really have been a town project. The council may have elected the dean but the accounts were kept strictly separate until the days of Riddoch. The Guildry's interest in the Tay ferries did not cease however with loss of ownership of Newport. In 1819 they expressed approval of a bill to improve the landing to allow steamboats to use the ferry. There had been complaints about its inconvenience and dangers, especially since improvements had been made to the Forth ferries. There were more travellers but most preferred a longer journey by land to the Woodhaven ferry rather than face the Tay crossing to Dundee.[18] After 1806, when, apparently largely through the exertions of the Berry family, a turnpike road was made joining the Cupar to Woodhaven road about four miles from Newport, the shorter distance began to attract more custom.[19] When it was discovered in 1819 that Lord Douglas, Lord Lieutenant of the county, who owned the right to ferry dues was prepared to give them up for both himself and his heirs 'to promote improvement of such utility to the public' the Guildry sent him a letter of thanks.

A few years later, they were active in protesting against William Berry of Tayfield, formerly Inverdovat, who was levying dues and seizing goods at Newport harbour.[20] The Guildry was very dubious about the legality of his actions and the dean was asked to press the town council to take court action against him. This case became somewhat drawn-out with the Guildry remaining enthusiastic, despite warnings that it would become very expensive.[21] Eventually the council asked for a contribution towards the expense as the case had been reluctantly undertaken only at their insistence.

As proprietors of land in Fife the Guildry became involved in the activities of the heritors there, and one which immediately affected their interests was the question of roads to the ferry, when they asked for and received help in 1713. The Fife Commissioners of Supply, who were responsible for road repairs were sufficiently interested at the start of the venture to give labour from adjacent lands. While not apparently attending many meetings, which he could and perhaps should have done, the dean asked later, in 1731, for a change of the line of a road to Newport by St Fort because of some enclosures he wanted to make. He meant to ensure that everything was done 'agreeable to law and not prejudicial to Newport'. In 1751, there was no doubt that a Guildry representative should attend a meeting at which the line of a new road was to be discussed. He hoped to persuade the commissioners that it should lead directly to Newport, which would be of great benefit to the ferry.[22] His expenses amounted to £14 19s and the 1753-54 accounts show £180 as having been paid to the Fife heritors to do as the Guildry asked.[23]

Other incidental responsibilities arose from ownership of the lands bought around the ferry, one almost immediately after the purchase of the adjacent lands in 1713. The stipend for parish ministers was paid largely from teinds – one tenth part of the rents – and in September the minister of St. Fillans church in Forgan parish, in which Newport was situated, summoned bailie Coupar – the tacksman – for augmentation of his stipend. Coupar was instructed to forward the summons to the Guildry at once and nothing more seems to have been heard of this. In 1728, the Guildry as heritors, who were then responsible for 'calling' ministers to a charge, were duly asked to attend a meeting to appoint a minister to the Forgan parish. They appointed Robert Pitcairn, a writer in Dundee, to represent them.[24] Parish ministers seem to be very long-living and this was the only record of their being so involved, but if they had had to pay for the services of a lawyer each time such attendance was required, it would have been yet another burden on their funds arising from their perhaps misguided venture into ferrying.

Another different sort of ferry attracted the attention of the Guildry in 1847. Only one member present at one meeting approved of the proposed ferry from Ferryport-on-Craig (Tayport) and Broughty Ferry.[25] The Edinburgh and Northern Railway Company had bought it to complete their route north, crossing by steam boats, and built a new harbour at Broughty. This had deleterious effects on the Newport ferry which the Dundee Harbour Trustees bought from the Caledonian Railway Company in 1873, but the railway bridge over the Tay affected it too. It was only when the motor car became supreme that the Newport ferry once again became a vital part of the Dundee transport system until in its turn it became obsolete when the Tay road bridge was opened in 1966.

NOTES

[1]   DCA; G1/2, 13-4-1713.
[2]   DCA; G1/2,2a, 8-2-1711, 26-9-1711.
[3]   DCA; G1/2, 21-9-1713.

4   DCA; G1/2, 26-4-1716, 24-1-1717.
5   DCA; G1/1, 6-5-1730, 23-7-1730.
6   DCA;G1/2, 9-5-1716, 17-5-1716.
7   DCA;G1/2, 7-4-1714.
8   DCA; G1/2, 24-10-1716.
9   DCA; TC56/2, f.16.
10 DCA; TC56/2, ff.10, 12.
11 DCA; TC56/2, ff.82, 83.
12 DCA; TC56/2, 1754.
13 DCA; G1/2, 8-3-1729.
14 DCA; TC56/2, 23-8-1749.
15 DCA; G3/2.
16 DCA;G3/2, 1782-3.
17 DCA; G1/4, 8.10.1782, but text damaged. Also Warden, 175-6.
18 DCA; G1/5, 25-2-1819.
19 NSA, ix, 512.
20 DCA; G1/5, 9-11-1825.
21 DCA; G1/6.
22 DCA; TC56/2, 27-5-1751.
23 DCA;G3/2, 1753-54.
24 DCA;G1/2, 7-11-1738.
25 DCA;G1/7, 11-2-1847.

10

THE GUILDRY AND
THE TOWN COUNCIL (1)

The town council and the Guildry had been inextricably linked since its origins. The dean was a member of the council *ex officio*, and a further member of the Guildry had been a councillor since 1642. The dean chaired the Dean of Guild Court whose jurisdiction had been confirmed by parliament in 1593,[1] and its records in the earlier part of the sixteenth century are mixed with those of the head court of the town. The town clerk acted as clerk to the Guildry. With the election of the dean in the hands of the town council, with the assessors mostly councillors, provosts and bailies, either past or present, it is hardly surprising that while reading the minutes of the Guildry meetings, particularly those of dean and his council, one gains the impression that those present did not wholly separate their roles. The town councillors, one must assume, could have had no doubt about their role, but when some of the same group of men, sometimes sitting in the council-house if not in the actual room where the council met, were acting as the assessors of the Guildry, their attitudes were perhaps less certain. Indeed, when the row broke out between Guildry and council in 1814-15 the question was once put to them as to how they conceived themselves when acting on behalf of the society.

This ambiguity in attitudes was not too surprising. As we have seen, the Guildry carried out many functions which can be described as those of local government. It has been argued that the burgh always had control of a guild within its boundaries and that the *Statutes of the Gild* had been passed by burgh authorities not by the guilds. Indeed, one historian has described the Merchants' Letter on which the Dundee Guildry based their case for total independence from the council in 1815 as merely a contract between council and guild, in effect its *Seal of Cause*, comparable to those awarded to the craftsmen's incorporations.[2] This is not an opinion that would have been welcomed by the Guildry in the early nineteenth century or by their historian, A.J. Warden.

However, with a council consisting largely of merchants it is unlikely that the basic commercial interests of the merchants were ever ignored, even if the council did appoint the dean with no reference to the Guildry. In addition, as the council had kept the Guildry's accounts separate from the town's, though the actual cash seems to have been handed over to the burgh treasurer, there must have been at least an illusion of independence. While the society itself retained control of entry of members and of its poor fund, and was reasonably satisfied with council policy, the Guildry seems to have been content with this arrangement – at least for a couple of centuries. Indeed, it was suggested that by 1800 it was probable that few of the guild brethren realised that they had ever had the right to elect their dean. In the small town of the seventeenth and the greater part of the eighteenth centuries, the number of guild brothers who would be enthusiastic or perhaps wealthy enough to undertake office would be limited.

Things changed, however, as the town grew; the membership of the Guildry increased with the town's population, and the wealth of individual merchants grew too. By the second half of the eighteenth century Dundee was flourishing in every aspect of life – economic, social and intellectual.[3] There was also a strong radical element in the town, as the ideas of the French Revolution spread, though perhaps not too widely among the comfortably off. Considerable unrest was experienced in 1792 when a Tree of Liberty was planted.[4] In addition 'one artful and ambitious individual', Alexander Riddoch, had cleverly obtained control of the town council and manipulated it to retain that control since the 1780s. It should be noted that he did nothing illegal in his methods of filling the council with men who were described as 'his own creatures'.[5] An act of parliament of 1469 had turned burgh councils into 'self-perpetuating oligarchies'.[6] One example will illustrate his methods. In September 1816, just before the annual elections, John Collier was admitted to the Guildry and made merchant councillor on the same day.[7] The members of the Guildry can hardly have welcomed the appointment of a totally new guild brother as their representative.

As Riddoch's abuse of power had became so blatant it was hardly surprising that he roused opposition. Many industrialists, radicals and merchants gradually came to believe that the town councillors displayed activity in town affairs only where their own interests were concerned. This was the more strongly felt because of the impotence of opponents to take any effective action to oust Riddoch. It must have been extremely frustrating for those excluded from official positions, who probably felt they were as able as many on the council, to have no part in managing the business of the town.

Some of the older among the Guildry brethren may also have been disturbed by the fact that general meetings of the society had practically ceased after 1792, when the minutes of the preceding year were copied word for word. The minutes until 1795 reported only appointments by nomination, whereafter there were no minutes at all until 1801 when only seven magistrates were present – and their purpose was to raise the ministers' stipends, for which the Guildry was partly responsible. The town had quietly taken control of the Guildry's funds. In 1807, at a meeting at which no names of those present appeared, the Guildry's fees were raised from £12 to £20. After that, apart from 'unsigned jottings' which raised the dean's officer's salary to £20, there was nothing of substance recorded until 1815 when a full meeting of the Guildry was called to elect members to the new Harbour Commission.[8]

The state of the harbour was the catalyst that aroused the dissatisfied to action. The upkeep of the harbour was the responsibility of the council but, always short of funds, it had always needed to be pressed to take enough action to maintain it, far less make the improvements the merchants thought it needed. From the late seventeenth century proposals for repairs and extensions were made to the council.[9] In 1718, 1721 and 1724 the council was being asked to repair or clean the harbour with money obtained from various sources such as Dundee's shore silver dues, from the other royal burghs, and from parliament.[10] In 1730 an act of parliament had entitled the council to levy 2d Scots on every Scots pint of ale or beer sold within the town, the money collected to be expended on clearing the town's debts and on harbour repairs, but the results were not impressive.

Between 1745 and 1791, largely due to the textile trade, import tonnage from foreign ports had increased from 1,280 to 10,520, while export had grown from 500 to 1,276.[11] Ships too had increased in tonnage, but the harbour's amenities had not been developed at a parallel rate. The council had spent most of the cash from the levy on trying to clear the town's debts and had done a little to improve harbour facilities – but not enough. In 1760 merchants had complained to the dean's court that the harbour was 'so very foul', filled up with so much mud that no vessels of 'any reasonable burden' could enter. The dean was instructed to ask the council to have the mud cleared.[12] The harbour could boast 3,000 feet of quays but it was still tidal and only 500 feet of quay space was available for vessels to berth – and they needed a full tide to float.[13] Furthermore, only about a quarter of harbour dues collected between 1764 and 1814 had been invested in improving the harbour despite the growth of the linen trade on which so much of Dundee's prosperity depended.[14]

Some credit has been attributed to Riddoch for what improvements were made up until that point, but economy in council expenditure was his main aim. By 1814, however, it was clear that Dundee needed more than a tidal harbour 'choked with mud'. When the council promoted a bill at Westminster which included almost as an afterthought the setting up of a commission to improve the harbour, which would have been completely under the control of the town council, opposition from practically all radical and commercial interests in the town erupted. A committee of merchants was formed, under the leadership of Robert Rintoul, editor of the *Dundee, Perth and Cupar Advertiser*, James Saunders, a solicitor, and David Blair, a linen merchant. With the help of the local M.P., the opponents of the bill were able to have a Harbour Act passed in 1815 under which the harbour was to be managed by a commission including seven town councillors and thirteen representatives from other interests in the town. This removed council control, and the added importance of this act for the Guildry was that they were recognised officially in the act for the first time as an incorporated body, and as such were allowed to elect four members of the commission. Not surprisingly this galvanised the Guildry into activity. Some of the brethren met and elected their four members even though the dean, David Brown (elected of course by the council) refused to call the necessary meeting on the grounds that he had been addressed as the 'nominal' dean.[15] It was pointed out that his presence was not necessary on the occasion when these commissioners were elected and that this was in accordance with the constitution of the Harbour Commission.

Such a successful display of independence clearly gave impetus to those who had previously seen no way to weaken Riddoch's power. What had been a 'vague tradition' that their incorporation had once been the most important body in the burgh, became a general topic of discussion, and a committee of twenty-one of their members was set up to ascertain the extent of their rights and in particular whether they could elect their own officers and manage their own funds. This committee's report was printed by Rintoul in 1815.[16] The extent of Riddoch's control was realised when it became known that the council not only kept the Guildry's records but that they were allowed no access to these. Indeed, as the town clerk was also the Guildry clerk it is easy to see how and why such a position was maintained.

Rintoul began to offer some public support to the campaign and quickly thirty guild brothers called a meeting at which a committee was appointed, with James Saunders as its clerk. The town council refused to recognise this group as official representatives of the Guildry, but on 3 March 1815 gave permission for the records of the Guildry to be made available for inspection. Ten days later, on 13 March, the Guildry's request that this should be done without any of the town council present was agreed to. But the council added defensively that they were not aware of having acted contrary to the set of the burgh or of having departed from the practice of their predecessors in election of the council. In this they were of course perfectly correct. They were on less secure ground when they claimed that they had not usurped the rights of the Guildry and Nine Trades.[17]

The Guildry decided to employ someone skilled in the art of reading ancient records to decipher them. This expert was George Home of the Register Office, Edinburgh, and he produced a veritable bombshell for the council in the shape of the Merchants' Letter and the subsequent royal charter. He also showed how rarely the Guildry had met in the last thirty years or so and how little business relating purely to Guildry matters had been dealt with. On 26 July, the praeses of the Guildry committee, George Clark, wrote to the council asking whether the magistrates were to approve or oppose the Guildry's resumption of the rights conferred on it by royal charter. The reply of 3 August from the council conceded that it was very proper for the Guildry to elect assessors, their collector and the officer and manage their own funds but as the Dean of Guild was a town councillor, he should be elected by the council. The council could not alter the set of the burgh without the authority of the Convention of Royal Burghs which did not meet until July 1816; therefore they would elect the dean this year and as David Brown's appointment had not been objected to by the Guildry he would remain in office until the next election.[18]

The council soon had a change of heart. Their intention to appeal to the Convention of Royal Burghs was seen by the Guildry as a definite threat and their suspicions were soon proved correct. At a meeting on 9 August the council confirmed that they would continue to elect the dean. The grounds on which they defended this decision was that it was so long since the Guildry's rights had been claimed that they did not think council recognition was sufficient, that while they had 'no intention of erecting a barrier' to these rights by applying to the Convention, as had been suggested, the dean's judicial function made it essential that he should be elected in such a manner that left 'no apprehension of doubt as to the legality of his acts'.

At the beginning of September some of the Guildry had called a general meeting and invited dean David Brown, to act as chairman, and to bring the minute book to the meeting. He not only refused to attend but had David Blair, junior, called out of the hall to tell him that under consultation - one can guess with whom – he did not think it prudent to give the minute book to the meeting. As the council had already agreed to hand over the Guildry's records and funds, one member suggested his conduct was censurable and disrespectful to the magistrates. The clerk of the meeting, still the town clerk, said that he could not advise the Guildry to follow a different course from that pointed out by the council, but the meeting nevertheless went ahead and appointed Robert Jobson as dean.

On 26 September 1815, the council leet for the dean included two names only, Andrew Peddie and George Thoms. On 28 September of all the deacons of the Trades summoned as usual to the elections, only the deacon of the Fleshers did not object to the election of various councillors: the other deacons disapproved of one on the grounds that he was collector of customs, another because he rented two public yards. They also declared that it was the Guildry's privilege to draw up the leet for the election of the dean - not the council's. They accused the council of having broken faith with the Guildry, and they added that Andrew Peddie too rented public ground on an illegal length on lease, and on too small a rent. No notice was taken, though the clerk did record all this in the council minutes. When the annual elections took place, Robert Jobson appeared, asking to be admitted as dean appointed by the Guildry. His request was refused by the council – unanimously, according to the council records, though it is unlikely that the Trades councillors voted against him – and the council nominee Andrew Peddie was declared elected.[19]

Thereafter relations between council and Guildry went from bad to worse. In November 1815 the incorporation found that their hall had been locked against them on the order of the magistrates and they gathered in the Exchange Coffee Rooms. When the dean met Provost Riddoch to ask why this had happened he replied that the magistrates disapproved of permitting the Guildry to assemble in the hall. There was no further explanation.[20] On 20 March 1816 the council met again – somehow managing to avoid the inconvenient presence of the Trades councillors – and revoked their original concessions to the Guildry, on a motion moved by Mr. David Blair, senior. This declared that the charter rights claimed by the Guildry had either never existed or had passed into desuetude – Scots laws which fell out of use became invalid – and that the earlier motion would unhinge the constitution and lead to anarchy. The Guildry decided to go to law. There was some consultation with the Perth Guildry whose lawyers had advised them that the Court of Session could not restore the rights of electing the dean because of more than forty years of a different practice. However, there was no doubt that the Guildry still might manage its own affairs. At a meeting in the Exchange Coffee Rooms they decided to obtain an act of declarator from the Court of Session to secure that right and also to claim that their funds had been grossly mismanaged. They would apply to parliament if the courts did not provide redress and collected subscriptions to fund their action.[21]

All the contenders in this disagreement had their own agenda (as has been shown in Provost Riddoch's biography), particularly James Saunders, the radical lawyer, who pushed the Guildry into action.[22] One letter in the *Dundee, Perth and Cupar Advertiser* claimed that he had 'inveigled' the Guildry into legal moves. As the meeting which was in favour of this course of action had an attendance of 150 it seems unlikely that some of the incorporation – having discovered what rights they once had – took much inveigling to try to restore these. When faced with the council's reneging on their first agreement to allow them some concessions (at a council meeting that was illegally convened in any case due to the omission of a summons to the Nine Trades), and finding themselves shut out of their hall, it is hardly surprising that tempers rose. The Dundee Trades were also understandably aggrieved by the contempt shown them by the council and their convener took every opportunity at council meetings to speak out in favour of the Guildry.

Considering what was happening at this time the atmosphere in the town in 1816 cannot have been pleasant. A letter in the *Advertiser* had prophesised only too well that if the council were so foolish as to renege on their promise to agree to the Guildry's demands they would arouse dissension in the town.[23] The venom expressed publicly in the local press, and presumably privately, demonstrated the strength of feeling in the town among those involved in the struggle. The council invariably referred to the committee of the Guildry as the 'so-called' committee. The Guildry referred to the council as Riddoch and his 'junto'. There were attacks on the individual councillors in the press. The Guildry advertised a meeting on 1 October to be held in the Guild Hall to elect their Dean. When they assembled they found the hall locked once more and removed to the Ancient Operative Masons' hall. There they received a Bill of Suspension imposing an interdict on them which forbade their meeting. They ignored this by declaring themselves a meeting of individuals.

At a meeting on 10 October with Patrick Anderson, the council's choice of dean was in the chair, despite protests voiced by David Blair, junior, whose father was a prominent Riddoch supporter. It emerged that the Bill of Suspension had been obtained not by the council officially but by a group of individuals, with Mr. Barrie carrying out the legal steps, and Blair's motion described them as people 'whose zeal for the public good was … questionable'. Provost Riddoch attended this meeting as a merchant and guild brother, and he and almost all the town councillors there voted against a resolution stating the Guildry's position. They were in the minority, however, and the meeting went on to make further resolutions for future action. A few days later James Ivory, an advocate, was appointed as their junior counsel.

The same day, 16 October 1816, John Baxter of Idvies and some other gentlemen offered their services as mediators in the name of a 'body of gentlemen anxious to restore peace and harmony' to the town. The subcommittee of the Guildry agreed to meet them and made it quite clear they maintained their view on such matters but were prepared to make one concession: that they would not hold a meeting planned for 23 October. The mediators met Provost Riddoch who received them 'very graciously' and thanked them for their efforts.

Discussions took place throughout October and November. The Guildry were advised to use more conciliatory language and informed that personal abuse had been prejudicial to their cause. The Guildry committee replied only that they would consider the advice of the mediators and at a meeting to attempt conciliation arranged by them on 24 October there was 'much polite talk'. The Guildry pointed out that they could recover their funds by law but thought it better that the magistrates agreed to this, but at the same time accepted blame for some of the ill-feeling of the past year. Provost Riddoch, however, confirmed the suspicions of all who may have doubted his sincerity in the matter by informing the meeting that he and his friends came 'not as magistrates' and therefore it would be premature to consider any pledge on behalf of the council. He suggested that the Guildry's claim should be put in writing and Messrs Anderson and Roberts could meet to discuss how this should be presented to the council. They duly did, but nothing happened, and Anderson stated that he wanted to wash his hands of the matter because of the delicacy of feeling.

Two Guildry members met one of the mediators, Mr. William Small, on 14 November to try to speed things up, as it was reported that some of the magistrates had been 'heard to express hostile sentiments' on the Guildry's prayer. The mediators met Riddoch that evening and evoked the comment from him that he was determined to hand on all the powers of the magistrates as he had found them. When Baxter remarked that in that case it was a pity he had troubled to meet the Guildry, he answered that not to have done so would have shown hostile temper to the public. When asked when he would call a meeting of the town council he gave the astonishing answer that he did not know: 'These gentlemen were very busy about their own affairs'. The mediators then decided that if there was no town council meeting by 25 November they would consider their negotiations with the magistrates at an end. Two days later, the Guildry committee thanked the mediators despite their total failure and it was decided to print the proceedings.

In the meantime a further complication had arisen. The Guildry's case against the council before the Court of Session had begun when it was generally thought that the action had been temporarily called off. James Saunders had sent the summons to the Edinburgh agents on 18 October, with the information that the current negotiations would probably render it unnecessary, but the Lords of Session had apparently not realised that further instructions would be needed before they began the proceedings. The council had received notice of this on 21 November, but it was thought that this would not have influenced the magistrates as Riddoch had already made his position crystal clear, and dean Anderson confirmed that the magistrates would not negotiate about the funds even though they had accepted Saunders' explanation that the action was called by mistake.

On 23 May 1817, the following year, the Court of Session indicted that it was inclined to favour the Guildry's case but wanted it put in writing. At the same time the Guildry petitioned the Convention of Royal Burghs, which recommended in July that the town council should be approached again, adding that the magistrates should adopt measures to restore peace.[24] The Convention reported that they could not decide the question and could see nothing in the council's decision of 9 August 1815 – when they had first agreed to the Guildry's requests – that was likely to 'unhinge the constitution'. But they did say that the decisions of that date should not have been rescinded without consulting the Nine Trades. The Guildry, the convener and deacons of the Nine Trades, with 126 guests, celebrated these reports at a dinner in the Sailors Hall.

Whether any approach to the magistrates at that time would have been successful immediately is perhaps doubtful. One of the criticisms made had been that they had failed to reappoint constables. Moreover, the Meal Mob riots of December 1816 had caused great alarm in the town and rather forced the issue. In June, at a meeting to renew the appointment of constables, Riddoch had reportedly flown into a 'paroxysm of rage' when the Guildry was mentioned and expressed himself in 'the most gross and beastly' of terms.[25] Then on 29 September 1817, a further petition from Mr. David Miln and several others 'calling themselves a committee of the Guildry' presented a petition which was ordered to lie on the table. As it commented on men 'so dead to the voice of reason', among other allegations regarding misconduct of the magistrates and council, this was not too surprising.[26]

A week later Patrick Whitson, the dean, protested that nothing should be done at the head court prejudicial to the ancient rights of the Guildry but deacon Mudie of the Nine Trades put various very pertinent questions. He asked whether the dean thought that the Guildry was or was not an incorporation, and in effect where lay the loyalties of assessors who were also town councillors. Riddoch actually moved that these questions should not be recorded in the council minutes but should be written on a separate piece of paper. The clerk advised Riddoch to withdraw his motion but the provost had not yet given up the fight. He claimed that the accounts were not yet audited so could not let the Trades see them. When Mr. John Crichton suggested that the resolution of 9 September 1815 should be carried into effect, Riddoch moved that more time was needed; and Riddoch's move was of course carried.

Within a week he had totally changed his tune. He proposed asking the king in council for a new set for the burgh, and his proposals were so liberal that, if followed, his reputation with posterity would indeed have been a very different one. He also proposed that the committees of the town council and the burgesses should meet to arrange the delivery of all the Guildry's funds, books and papers to a dean and assessors chosen by them. A *volte face* indeed. The change was determined by the fact, as deacon Hogg reported to the Guildry in December 1817, that the council had been ordered by the Court of Session to hand over everything belonging to the Guildry including titles to lands and other heritable subjects.[27] The town had to borrow £1,000 from the Ferguson mortification to pay off the Guildry,[28] and there were other financial arrangements to be made. A bond by the kirk fabric had to be assigned to the Guildry and in the end much of their capital was left in the hands of the council, with interest of 4½% or 5%, bringing in an income for the Guildry poor. What had happened to all their funds when the council controlled them was a mystery.

After the long bitter fight the Guildry was for the first time in over 200 years empowered to make its own choice of dean, and to appoint assessors who were not town councillors. The following year, on 28 September 1818, a meeting was called in the Guild Hall to elect their officers and if it was found too small for a large attendance they would adjourn to the South Kirk where the vestry had been their usual meeting place in earlier times. They celebrated their independence by deciding to buy a chain for the dean to be worn at the first meeting of the council after his election.[29] They wrote to John Wilson, a merchant in London, and after the design was determined requested that it was to be made of the very best standard of gold, on a budget of 50-60 guineas.[30] The accounts of 1818-1819 show that the final cost was £67 3s 6d (plus 1s 2½d postage).[31] The chain has been worn since by the deans on all official occasions. Another signal of the Guildry's new-found independence was a seal, bought in 1819 for £6 6s.[32]

NOTES

[1]   *APS.* iv, c.30.

[2]   Murray, i, 464.

[3]   C. Mckean, 'Not even the trivial grace of a straight line – or why Dundee never built a new town', in L. Miskell, C.A. Whatley and B. Harris (eds.), *Victorian Dundee* (2000), 19-20.

[4]   K.J. Logue, *Popular Disturbances in Scotland, 1780-1815* (Edinburgh, 1979), 149-52.

[5]   E. Gauldie, *One Artful and Ambitious Individual* (Dundee, 1989), 20-21.

[6]   *APS*, ii, 95 c.5.

[7]   DCA; DTC, Book 15, 24-9-1816.

[8]   DCL; Lamb, 195 (i) *Report by Committee Appointed to ascertain the Ancient Rights of the Guildry*; G1/4, 11-2-1815.

[9]   Warden, 159-160.

[10]   DCA; G1/2, 3-2-1712, 11-1-1718, July 1721, 2-7-1724.

[11]   B. Lenman, *From Esk to Tweed* (Glasgow, 1975), 27.

[12]   DCA; TC56/2, 8-4-1760.

[13]   Lenman, *From Esk to Tweed*, 74.

[14]   W. Kenefick, 'The Growth and Development of the Port of Dundee', in Miskell *et al.* (eds.), *Victorian Dundee*, 40-41.

[15]   DCL; Lamb, 195 (i).

[16]   DCL; Lamb, 195 (i).

[17]   DCA; DTC,.Book 14, 4-3-1815.

[18]   DCA; DTC, Book 14, 3-8-1815.

[19]   DCA; DTC, Book 14 , 28-9-1815, 3-10-1815.

[20]   DCA; G1/4b.

[21]   DCA; G1/4b, 3-4-1816, 20-5-1816.

[22]   Gauldie, *One Artful and Ambitious Individual*, 47,48.

[23]   DCL; *Dundee, Perth and Cupar Advertiser*, 15-9-1815.

[24]   DCL; *Advertiser*, 11-7-1817.

[25]   DCL; *Advertiser*, 11-4-1817.

[26]   DCA; DTC, Vol.15, 29-9-1817.

[27]   DCA; G1/4, December 1817.

[28]   DCA; G1/4, 3-12-1817.

[29]   DCA; G1/4, 28-9-1818, 30-9-1818.

[30]   DCA; G4/1, 16-10-1818.

[31]   DCA; G3/3, 1818-1819.

[32]   DCA; G1/5, 3-9-1819.

11

THE GUILDRY AND
THE TOWN COUNCIL (2)

This battle with the town council was won but it cannot be pretended that all was sweetness and light thereafter. The radicals would not be satisfied until they had achieved political reform. The town council could not have been best pleased when the Guildry accepted a motion that the incorporation should resume the practice of offering the magistrates advice,[1] and even less pleased when their choice of shoremaster was criticised. The Guildry complained that he was ignorant of nautical affairs, and he was declared an enemy of the rights and privileges of his fellow citizens. In addition he was already stampmaster and, as he had to carry out those duties personally, he had no time for public duties. Then they added that if the council 'mean to preserve themselves as a separate body, they will imitate their predecessors', but if they wished to be more liberal and enlightened they would consult the Guildry and the Nine Trades.[2] An entry in the *Advertiser*, a *Prolegemon* by R. Distaffeus noted that 'A council from corruption sprung remains corrupted still'.[3]

There can be little doubt that a certain amount of pettiness had been shown on all sides during the bitter dispute. One example was shown in May 1815 when a meeting of the Guildry was called specially to discuss whether they should walk in the procession with other public bodies for the good of the infirmary. Only the comment that the managers of the hospital seemed to think that it was a benefit to the institution persuaded them to forget their general 'disapproval of processions'.[4] Provost Anderson had alleged at a meeting of the head court in the autumn of 1818 that the resolutions of the Guildry and the Nine Trades had been adopted for the purpose of insulting the magistrates and the town council. It was considered pertinent by the Guildry that he had made no attempt to vindicate the selection of councillors objected to by them and the Nine Trades.[5] The anomaly of the position of councillors who were also guild brothers is illustrated on this occasion by the resolution of a general meeting of the Guildry, that Provost Anderson should be censured at the next meeting he attended for his adverse comments of what was after all his association.[6]

The convener of the Nine Trades on the other hand had been congratulated at an earlier general meeting of the Guildry on the 'manly manner and ability' with which he had opposed the 'abettors of a system which excluded the most respectable, independent and public-spirited citizens' from the management of town affairs.[7] The Nine Trades had been vocal and active in defending both the Guildry's and their own rights throughout the struggle with the council, refusing to approve accounts, for instance. It would be a long time before the ill-feeling of those years would disappear or even be lessened.

During the early part of 1818 the question of changes in burgh government continued not only in the Guildry but among some of the burgesses who were not happy with the current state of affairs. In March 1818 the outcome of a meeting of burgesses was reported which wanted a committee to collaborate with the town council, the Guildry and the Nine Trades to draw up a petition to the Convention of Royal Burghs. Unfortunately, as Mr. Robert Mudie had made remarks which were interpreted as reflecting badly on the magistrates, Riddoch refused to become a member with the result that all the other councillors refused initially to accept nomination until he eventually agreed to tell the town clerk to cooperate. In April criticisms of a parliamentary bill on burgh reform were made, giving the reasons for the Guildry's views, as well as proposals for improvements. These were then sent to the Lord Advocate, the Convention of Royal Burghs, the Nine Trades and every Guildry in Scotland. Lord Archibald Hamilton promised to present the Guildry's view on the matter of burgh reform to the House of Commons at the first opportunity.[8]

The magistrates and the Nine Trades in the meantime had been preparing a petition to the Convention of Royal Burghs, the draft of which the Guildry approved and supported by their own petition. There were actually doubts as to whether any changes could be made except by act of parliament, although in 1709 the Convention had made changes. A copy of the new set reached them in August 1818. Three of the twenty-one councillors were to be elected by the Guildry and the Trades, and as a result on 29 September 1819 the Guildry elected David Blair, junior, who had been active throughout the campaign on the incorporation's behalf, as dean and William Roberts, a banker, as the Guildry councillor.[9] The oath they were asked to take illustrated clearly some of the sins of which previous councils were believed to be guilty. They had to swear to elect and appoint magistrates and teachers they considered best qualified; to refuse to allow public property to be let by private bargains; not to vote for borrowing by the council unless they were sure it was for the good of the town; and not to allow their personal interest to sway their votes. A councillor representative of the Nine Trades was also to be elected by that body.

The following year another bill to reform burgh government was before parliament and was less warmly received than the previous bill presented in 1818. In addition, the Guildry complained bitterly that the House of Commons was being misled, first into believing that the burgesses really aimed at parliamentary reform, and secondly that only a small number of the burgesses, who were 'not the most respectable' among them, had applied for reform, In fact, they claimed that four fifths of the burgesses owning nine tenths of property liable to be affected by the magistrates' actions were in favour of reform and indeed, a petition sent to the Commons had the support of 450 burgesses.[10] The Guildry decided to appoint a committee to attend the House of Commons committee and to collect private subscriptions to assist this. The Nine Trades were to be consulted to discover if a joint committee would be acceptable.[11]

At the same time the attack on what was considered misgovernment by the council continued. At a meeting of the head court the Nine Trades had objected to the short leet for magistrates put forward by the council and threatened to refuse permission for any borrowing if this protest was ignored. There was annoyance when it was stated that Bailie John Calman had alleged that 'the honest trades' had been taken possession of by three or four of the Guildry who made 'catspaws' of them.[12] In great indignation, the Guildry sent a petition to the council emphasising that as an incorporation the Guildry was satisfied with the set but as individuals they thought more 'intensive' change was necessary.[13] At the meeting the point was also made that while it was true that members of the Guildry and the Trades were not entitled to interfere in elections, the only organs through which they could express their views were their incorporations. It was suggested that their recommendations should therefore be accepted, instead of the council bringing in totally unknown persons and others 'declared enemies of the liberal system proposed by Provost Riddoch'! The petition however had to be printed at the expense of James Saunders, the clerk to the Guildry, an avid radical, as some members felt they needed greater acquaintance with the contents of the petition.

The editor of the *Dundee, Perth and Cupar Advertiser*, Mr. Rintoul, was sent to London to represent the Guildry in discussions on the bill for burgh reform and his report came before the Guildry in August 1819.[14] Recuperating from a serious illness he had accepted the remit somewhat unwillingly but was ready to do so without any payment except his expenses. He had laboured under some disadvantages. He was aware that some of the complaints made against the council would have seemed petty to strangers. Indeed the parliamentary report remarked on the 'petty scale' of the various peculations.[15] Perhaps it took a local Dundonian to appreciate how 'many a mickle' had in fact become a 'muckle' (several decades of 'mickles' under the influence of one man had become a very big 'muckle' indeed in the eyes of many burgesses). In addition, very few Dundee tradesmen had been able to remain in London as the time taken over the investigation into the situation in Dundee lengthened – although dean Jobson had made some effective comments on the obscurity surrounding the financial dealings of the council, especially where the Guildry's funds were concerned. Provost Riddoch on the other hand had been able to spend the whole time there, acting as if he were on holiday, and when the report of the Select Committee did appear, it was felt it was based almost wholly on his evidence.[16]

Unpleasantly for Rintoul, an anonymous letter had been sent to Lord Archibald Hamilton accusing him of misdemeanours. Lord Hamilton did not inform Rintoul of this until he had made sure the accusations were unfounded. Though the bill did not become law, the Guildry were sufficiently satisfied with Rintoul's services to give him the freedom of the Guildry.[17] And when the M.P. for Montrose, Mr. Hume, passed through Dundee the Nine Trades invited the Guildry to their hall to receive him so that he too could be thanked for his services.[18]

Further disagreements arose between council and Guildry in September 1819, when a general meeting of the Guildry decided to exercise its right as burgesses to attend the election of the magistrates. This of course was something they had not done for many years. They assembled at 11 a.m. and made for the hall where the election was being held. The town officer, acting under the orders of Provost Anderson, refused to admit them. Later they were informed by the Guildry councillor, who was of course there in his official capacity, that there had been a motion to admit the burgesses but all the self-elected councillors had voted against this.[19] In December it was decided to take legal advice in conjunction with the Nine Trades as to whether the council could refuse to record protests against their proceedings, but it seems that this was not followed up.[20]

In October 1819 a very sarcastic entry appeared in the report of the general meeting of that month.[21] The offices of kirkmaster, held by George Thoms, and that of chamberlain by Bailie Patrick Whitson had been demitted by these men. The Guildry commented that if these resignations had taken place as admissions of the soundness of the incorporation's opinions against members of the council holding places of emolument under themselves (in other words 'acting as master and servant') then it was worthy of praise. However, the report continued that if – coupled with the joining of these offices into one with the salary of £100 p.a. – the two men were merely forwarding the appointment of Thom's son, Mr. P.H. Thoms, to this lucrative situation, then the transaction must be regarded as a 'job'. If so then this was offensive to the public, a disgrace to the projectors, and a dishonour to the person who should accept. Such attacks did not make for better relations between Guildry and council, whether justified or not.

There was a minor squabble over the sallies' attendance at funerals. In 1826 the dean was asked to propose to the council that the Guildry should either have the right to appoint them or the council should do so, and also pay the expense of clothing them.[22] The sallies were paid for their attendance at funerals which meant that the council was annexing another form of patronage. The accounts indicate that the Guildry won this particular little fight.

The general atmosphere in the country was not in favour of reform of any kind in the years after Waterloo. In 1824 there was even a move by the government officials to return the set of 1819 to its previous form, a move which the Guildry thought would disturb the peace of Dundee – such as it was.[23] In 1825 the council had plans for improving Dundee but this also ran into opposition, which the Guildry expressed forcibly. There was still bitterness about the decision in 1793 to sell the hospital, the charitable institution – very much against popular opinion – and to allow the use of its grounds and the money gained to lay out new streets. This move had ignored the legal powers of the Trades and the Guildry, where selling town property was concerned. The council's refusal in 1825 to countenance a clause to extend the jurisdiction of the Dean of Guild's court to the expanded royalty roused more wrath, although not everyone approved of that court.[24]

The issue of harbour improvement was to cause more trouble in 1829 and 1830. The Harbour Commission intended to apply for a bill to extend the docks and reduce the shore dues, which the Guildry agreed was necessary.[25] The town council, however, decided to oppose the bill, and their decision to suggest using £3,000 of public money for this purpose was also roundly and strongly criticised.[26] Opposition was roused all over the county as well as in the burgh, as it appeared that the council was attempting to regain control of the harbour. The opposition was so strong that an act of Parliament vested control of the harbour in a Harbour Trust, while the council merely received compensation for any resulting losses. The Guildry on the other hand had obtained direct influence on the management of the harbour as they were in future to elect four trustees from their own membership.[27] As a result harbour matters appear regularly thereafter in their discussions.

The disagreement which had the most far-reaching effect occurred in 1827. The council had had to receive the dean and Guildry and Trades councillors elected by their incorporations since 1819, however much they disliked the choices made. In October 1827, after a very close contest (which because of a large turn-out of 269 involved a move to the Cross Church to accommodate all the guild brothers who wished to vote), the Guildry elected Alexander Kay. He had 141 votes against the 128 cast for William Lindsay. The town council refused to accept Kay on the grounds that he was a burgess only for life. They contemptuously called him a 'burgee' which the Chambers dictionary defines as 'a swallow-tailed flag or a kind of small coal for furnaces', and appointed Mr. Lindsay. There they made a dire error. By making Lindsay the dean, the council signed their own death warrant, and by refusing the dean and the guild councillor access to the town records they did nothing to help their cause.[28]

The Guildry with other groups interested in reform became very active in trying to rid the burgh of its self-perpetuating oligarchy, even sending a deputation to London which met Sir Robert Peel, who, it was reported, received them 'most graciously'. The various bodies were ready to pay for all of this activity and were rewarded eventually. In 1830 the result of an appeal to the Court of Session brought the decision that the council had been disfranchised from the time they rejected Kay, and from that point all their actions were deemed illegal. The House of Lords confirmed the Court of Session's decision. An election ordered by royal warrant, the electors to be burgesses and resident heritors took place on 10-12 May, 1831 and those promising to work to reform the system of electing councils soundly defeated those in favour of the status quo by 467 votes to 28 (out of a total of 765 voters). But the results of the election were disputed by the losers. Their case was heard before sheriffs in

Edinburgh who replaced three of the new council – the dean of Guild, the Guildry councillor and the convener of the Nine Trades – who had each received over 400 votes – with three supporters of the old regime whose popular support have been insignificant. The new council refused to accept this and sent a petition to the Privy Council. This was remitted to the Lord Advocate, who confirmed the election of the three deposed by the sheriffs' court. The council then elected Mr. Kay as dean, the Guildry having been deprived of that power by the set allowed by the Privy Council.[29] Until the act reforming all burgh council was passed in 1833 the Guildry had to put up with a council-appointed dean once more.[30]

Though initially it had been proposed to abolish the rights of all the guildries throughout Scotland in this act, Dundee and a few other towns managed to retain their privileges with the condition that these would be lost if the number of their members dropped to one quarter of what they were in 1833. From then until 1975 when local government in Scotland was completely altered, the Dundee Guildry continued to elect their dean who sat *ex officio* on the council, and chaired his court which dealt with property matters. In those burghs whose Guilds lost this power or had no Guildry at all, the dean was chosen from the town council.

Other difficulties arose on occasion between council and Guildry. The Guildry still met in their hall, a room on the first floor of the town house designed by William Adam. As we have seen the two rooms on that floor seem to have been exchanged between council and Guildry at some time. The west room was certainly marked in Adam's plans as Gilderyroom and its being offered as a store room for grain by the Guildry in the eighteenth century would seem to show that it was certainly the Guild Hall then, but several references make it clear that in the nineteenth century the east room was at that time used as their meeting place. In 1828, the only accommodation the council could offer the new sheriff-substitute appointed for Forfarshire was the Guild Hall. He was reported as holding his court there and the Guildry adjourned to the west hall, which seems to indicate that the east hall was at that time the Guild Hall. [31]

In 1862, the dean and the clerk had been asked to investigate the rights of the incorporation to the east hall, 'commonly called the Guild Hall'.[32] Some discontent had been rumbling on about their accommodation for some years within the Guildry. Worry about the safety of their records led to a demand for fireproof storage in 1848. In 1854 the skylight, the only window in their store room in the attic, had been closed up during some repairs to the roof and in consequence it was useless for the purpose of storing records. The dean was to try to have it opened or to obtain another suitable place.[33] There were complaints at intervals about the state of the hall. In 1829 there was a request that the council should have it washed and in 1864 not only was it described as 'much requiring cleaning', it was stated that it was unsatisfactory and uncomfortable.[34]

Faced with the report from the Guildry regarding their position regarding the hall, and perhaps a little disgruntled by their complaints, particularly in 1864 when these comments were made about its condition, the town clerk began to query their right of access to it. In April 1865 he wrote to the dean very firmly. He reminded him that to prevent misapprehension, the town council expected that if the dean and his assessors meant to assert a right to any part of the town house – 'contrary to the terms of my report' – then they must lay before the council a statement of the claim, with the evidence to support it.[35] However, the Guildry were still meeting in the Guild Hall in 1871,[36] although a committee to look at the claims to the Guild Hall was reappointed in 1873.[37] The Guildry presumably managed to convince the council then that they had a right to the use of the hall. Once the Adam town house was demolished, the Guildry moved with them and today they still meet in some part of the council buildings.[38]

NOTES

[1]   DCA; G1/4, 28-9-1818.
[2]   DCA; G1/4, 2-10-1818.
[3]   DCL; Lamb, 195(8).
[4]   DCA; G1/4, 27-5-1818.

[5]   DCA; G1/5, 26-10-1818.

[6]   DCA; G1/5, 26-10-1818.

[7]   DCA; G1/5, 5-10-1818.

[8]   DCA; G1/4, 27-5-1818.

[9]   DCA; G1/5, 29-9-1819.

[10] DCA; G4/1, 1819.

[11] DCA; G1/5, 3-5-1819.

[12] DCA; G1/5, 20-1-1819.

[13] DCL; Lamb, 195 (6).

[14] DCA; G1/5, 11-8-1819

[15] Quoted in Gauldie, *One Artful and ambitious Individual*, 52.

[16] DCA; G1/5, 29-9-1819.

[17] DCA; G1/5. 17-5-1819.

[18] DCA; G1/5, 4-5-1820.

[19] DCA; G1/5, 23-9-1819.

[20] DCA; G1/5, 29-12-1819.

[21] DCA; G1/5, 13-10-1819.

[22] DCA; G1/5, 26-12-1826.

[23] DCA; G1/5, 2-8-1824, 3-7-1827.

[24] DCL; Lamb, 195 (23).

[25] DCA; G1/6, 6a,14-10-1829.

[26] DCA; G1/6, 6a, 17-2-1830.

[27] 11 GIV, c.119.

[28] DCA; G1/6, 6a, 14-10-1829.

[29] DCL; Lamb 195(23).

[30] 3 & 4 WIV c.76.

[31] DCA; G1/6a, 4-10-1828.

[32] DCA;G1/7, 24-9-1862.

[33] DCA; G1/7, 19-7-1854.

[34] DCA; G1/8, 28-12-1864.

[35] DCA; G8/10, 5-4-1865.

[36] DCL; Lamb 195(25).

[37] DCA; G1/8, 26-11-1873.

[38] Information from Mr. David Goodfellow and Mr. Dennis F. Collins.

12

THE END OF PRIVILEGE

The Guildry were not to know that their hard-won independence from the council was to be of importance to them for such a comparatively short time. The desire for political reform, first experienced in the late eighteenth century and in the wake of the French Revolution, had gathered impetus in the 1820s and 1830s with the result that both parliamentary and burgh electoral lists were widened. By the 1840s there was growing demand for free trade between nations and the removal of restrictions within Britain. The Guildry shared in some of the action. At the end of 1830 they expressed general disapproval of the current parliamentary system, and in March 1831 a general meeting decided to petition parliament in favour of passing reform bills.[1] A resolution against the Corn Laws was approved as early as 1826, as the price of food was so high,[2] and in 1841 a petition for their total abolition was presented to parliament with copies being sent to the press.[3] They were less enthusiastic, initially at least, about any suggestion that their privileges within the burgh should be abolished. One reason for this was quite logical. The Guildry had legal financial obligations such as paying their share of the Dundee ministers' stipends. The question of how they could maintain these without the income from fees, fines, etc. was one which did worry them. At one point a list was made of just how much they had to honour which gave the incorporation food for thought.

Their privileges were undoubtedly restrictive but the incorporation continued to pursue offenders vigorously as long as they were in existence. Whether the time and money spent on this was really worthwhile is doubtful. The accounts for 1831 which were audited on 22 February 1832 showed an excess of expenditure over income of £115 12s 8½d, which was explained by the increasing prosecution of the unfree as well as a larger pension list.[4] Despite this evidence, in April 1833 it was proposed that the clerk should take legal action against some of those 'encroachers' to compel them to observe the Guildry's rules – he was to make sure that they paid the full dues of their freedom to compensate for the expense to which they had 'uselessly subjected the incorporation'.[5]

This last motion is especially interesting as a general meeting had been called a short time before this to discuss a motion to send a petition to both houses of parliament asking for the abolition of exclusive privileges of corporations. One member, a Mr. McEwan, had given notice of his intention to put forward this proposal, a procedure used by members when they intended to bring up some specially contentious issue. However, at the actual meeting he moved delay as it was believed that the Lord Advocate was about to bring forward bills to improve Scottish burghs generally and to empower the king to set up royal commissions of enquiry into abuses in several royal burghs.[6] Dundonians by this time perhaps realised that they had not been the only people who felt that their town councils could be improved. While the motion does show that some guild brethren were beginning to have doubts about their privileged position, at this point, the general meeting was ready only to appoint a committee to investigate any abuses of Guildry privileges and to order the dean and his assessors to examine any future bills which altered corporations in Scotland's royal burghs.[7] In the meantime, until abolition became a reality in 1846, all offenders were liable to find themselves, even as late as 1845, facing fines if they did not obtain licences or join the incorporation.

By the time the act removing all these long-established burgh and incorporation privileges was passed, there was more general acceptance of the need for change. The bill was examined and generally approved at a meeting in February 1846. Thereafter the dean and assessors had to consider what changes would have to be made as the incorporation's circumstances would be substantially altered. There was some justification for any resistance in the Guildry to altering the system. As well as paying a proportion of the stipends, the dean was a magistrate with his own court and procurator fiscal who had to be paid, and they recognised at least their moral duty to care for their own poor and sick. Once trade and business privileges were lost, there was little obvious material benefit to be gained from becoming a guild brother. It was possible for members to hope for a pension in case of sickness or poverty-stricken old age, but that could not be guaranteed and would certainly not be enormous. In fact one of the first necessary economies decided on, in May 1846, was the reduction in pensions; fourteen names were removed from their list and fifty-two were to receive less than a third of the sum previously allotted to them. The income expected once the bill was passed was just over £75. Out of that the Guildry were due £35 7s 3¾d for stipends and £53 4s 4d for salaries.[8] Before this date, the amount available to them had varied, but by the period 1770-1771 this increased from £548 to £1,661 in 1790-1791.[9] Income would still accrue from the letting of seats in the churches, from any property and from money lent out, but no longer could so much be expected from new entrants and of course nothing at all from fines (while fees could be problematical).

Faced with the drop in a regular income the incorporation was nothing if not realistic. Entry fees were reduced in an attempt to encourage merchants and others to join, admittedly without immediate success. At the beginning of August £5 was set for what was called 'full participation', sons-in-law were to pay £1 5s and 1s became the lifetime fee. Entrants still had to pay fees to the clerk and officer, and these were fixed at the next meeting as 3s 6d to the clerk, and 1s 6d to the officer.[10] However, the realisation that the Guildry still had a part to play in Dundee began a revival. In 1863 there were over thirty new members. In 1864 it was reported that there were 249 guild brethren and in 1870 thirty-one joined and of these only seven were for their life only.[11] All through the Guildry's history, though their main object was the protection of those monopolistic privileges for which members had paid to share, they had never neglected their duties as ordinary citizens. They used their organisation as a useful tool for making opinions known, for pressing for improvements to their town, and their position on the town council plus the financial aid they had given over the centuries to the town did strengthen any such pressure.

This attitude was not to change, but it is perhaps worth noting that until the nineteenth century, their records, like those of all the local societies, were almost completely silent on international events and important domestic issues, unless trade was directly affected. Events in the royal family might be mentioned, especially in the nineteenth century but almost all passed without comment as they occurred. The Union of the Crowns, the 1707 union of the parliaments, the Jacobite rebellions, numerous wars and conflicts, all passed unrecorded. The economic effects of 1715 did evoke an approach to the Convention of Royal Burghs asking if the burgh could be free from taxes because of the damage it had suffered, and there was also a query about the whereabouts of some of the town's cannon that had been removed to Perth,[12] but little else of substance.

The part of the Guildry's archive in which this silence is broken is rather a surprising one. In the minutes of the Convivial Society, which was founded in 1841, the clerk took it upon himself, for some reason, and in the first few years of its existence, to insert information and sometimes comments on outside events of greater or less importance. In 1843 the demolition of the old church was remarked on: it was noted that the 600-year-old walls were disappearing. The only comment so far found in all the Guildry archive on the Disruption that had such a profound effect on Scottish society was made in May 1843, and even then it was merely noted that it was generally regretted. Indeed, this was followed by the comment that the weather was cold and 'incongenial'. The dismissal of the French assembly by Louis Napoleon, president of France; the launching of the 'Harkaway', the largest vessel built by that time in Scotland, by Mr. Alexander Steven in Dundee; Wellington's death; the 1853 gold rush to 'that auriferous land', Australia; an earthquake on an island in the Caribbean; the arrest of a superintendent of the police in Dundee on a charge of fraud in Yorkshire; are only a few of the national and international events the clerk thought merited inclusion in the minutes.

When one looks at the nature of the Convivial Society, this exception to the general nature of the records becomes even more astonishing. As a rule the Guildry did not indulge in formal socialising, at least not in any way which would deserve entry in the minutes. The dinner to celebrate winning their case against the council was an exception. However, not long after the annual elections nine members met on 27 October for a meal and the Convivial Society was formed, and Mr. John Mair offered to 'give the next entertainment' – that is to pay for the next evening. As he said, he had been an assessor for a year but had not had the opportunity to do so before, it would appear that social gatherings of assessors were not an unusual occurrence. What this meeting set out to do was to make such meetings regular. A handsome leather volume in a leather case with a lock, now broken, bound by Mr. John Durham, a stationer and bookbinder in the High Street, was presented by Mr. David Anderson, as a minute book for the new society on 29 November.[13]

As the society had been formally organised before this the rules and regulations were altered once or twice before the minute book was formally opened, the first entry on two pages laid down the rules before any minute of earlier meetings and thirty-one members signed it. The reason given for forming the society was that the past year had shown that social intercourse among the dean and his assessors had contributed 'not only to the maintenance of friendly feeling but materially forwarded the interests of the incorporation'. The members were to consist of the dean, the assessors, the procurator fiscal of the guild court, the collector and the clerk; no member was to introduce any person who was not a member. Each year, after the annual elections, the dean was to be responsible for the entertainment of members at 'such a place as he shall name'. At the next meeting the newest assessor was 'in like manner' to entertain members, followed by each new assessor in order of his nomination. After each assessor had done so every member had to pay his share whether he was present or not!

Significantly, although it was decreed that the object was to promote and cultivate good feeling it was also stressed that these social events should not be extravagant affairs. This was no doubt to keep costs within reasonable limits and prevent rivalry among hosts. No discussion of religion or politics was allowed and the bill was to be called for at 11 p.m. The last regulation laid down that fines could be imposed if any of the rules was breached, to be paid to the collector for the benefit of the convivial funds of the society (as we shall see keeping this rule became farcical). The clerk was in fact the first person to be fined although oddly not for any breach of the Convivial Society's rules. He had not called the ordinary meeting of the dean and assessors for the proper night, and the following month had to pay 5s.

Meetings were usually held in taverns: the Royal hotel; the Fleece tavern; Fyall's Fifeshire tavern; and Wallace's Star Inn in the Murraygate are only a few of those patronised by the society. The locations, despite the rule against extravagance, may help to explain what can only be described as the early growth of frivolity in the proceedings. Or perhaps the other rule that any fines paid went towards the cost of the entertainment contributed to the increase in fines combined with the decrease in any seriousness in their application. One member would be fined one night for calling for the bill, while another, who clearly wanted home, was fined for reminding the dean to call for the bill. One insinuated that the florin (2s) of another member, Mr. Duncan, was a 'bawbie' (a halfpenny), to which Mr. Duncan took umbrage, arguing that this implied that he could not afford to pay his fine. The dean was also fined for joking, and fines were imposed for unsuccessful proposals intended to fine other members. Another member was fined for laughing too much, and a Mr. Webster was fined – justifiably one feels – for introducing a bear into the proceedings.

There was a short break in the life of the society between 1859 and 1861, when in November it was reported that the society had spent a happy afternoon, a change from evening dinners, 'heightened no doubt by a liberal quantity of choice wine' contributed by the dean. The November meeting became an annual event with the dean seeming to provide the wine on each occasion. Evening meetings were resumed for a time and then in 1880 the gathering began to meet at 5 p.m. Two years later, in February 1882, it is a little ironic to find the meeting giving enthusiastic approval to the success of the Gospel Temperance movement, when 35,000 had taken the pledge. The number of members who might have signed up for temperance was not recorded.

Any mention of public events disappeared from the twentieth century meetings and hilarity became the norm. In fact on one occasion the whole company was fined 'for being so very funny'. One would be fined for wearing evening dress, then at a later meeting for not doing so. One left to preside at a meeting about the docks and was fined for preferring God to Mammon. Members were clearly having a great time.

The last meeting recorded in the minute book was held on 20 October 1938 when the clerk pointed out that various heinous offences during meeting met with instant retribution in the shape of severe pecuniary fines. He hastened to add that all had been paid with alacrity, generally in threepenny bits. This coin was similar to today's fivepenny piece so it can be imagined how much fun that process must have engendered.

Such frivolity was of course out of place in the normal proceedings of the incorporation when the members' attention focussed, as it so regularly did throughout its history, on matters of importance to their society and to that of the town. For instance, the maintenance of law and order had always been of great concern. As burgesses, guild brothers were always due to help with watch and ward in the burgh, and throughout the centuries they were regularly involved in helping to keep the peace. On 16 March 1699, the dean and assessors met the magistrates, with the deacon convener of the Nine Trades and all the craft deacons, to discuss how they could prevent a repetition of riots that had occurred the night before. The dean recommended that the magistrates should appoint a commanding officer for each street to organise keeping a guard and should then discharge him when they thought necessary.[14] The suggestions made in the scroll minutes were much fiercer but were not endorsed in the minutes proper. The dean and his court had initially suggested that the 'instrumenters and fomentors' of the riot or of any future such incident should be treated as guilty of treason. Also they reckoned that any traders bringing food into the town should be protected and compensated by the authorities for any loss they suffered.[15] In 1817 they were very critical of the council for neglecting to appoint new constables, and in 1819 members of the Guildry were allotted to different districts to help with watch and ward. The following year a meeting was called especially to discuss the new police regulations set up. Approval was given and it was agreed that both as individuals and as a body the Guildry would support them fully.[16] In 1832, however, they refrained from expressing any views on a new Police Act, until there was a general meeting of the inhabitants of the burgh. Police at that time were concerned not only with keeping the peace but with physical conditions within burghs.

From the later seventeenth century, substantial assistance was given to the provision of education, practical and cultural, within the burgh. In 1697, the council asked for help in paying at least part of the salary of the writing master 'in respect of the town's low condition'. This salary was £6 sterling and the Guildry agreed to pay him £30 Scots (the Scots pound being worth one twelfth of sterling, so this amounted to £2 10s). A few years later in 1700 this arrangement was continued for David Ogilvie.[17] In the late 1690s, and again from 1712-22, they contributed £39 Scots to support a music master. Alexander Scott was appointed at the latter date and the Guildry continued to pay up when Mr. Scott left, asking only that his successor, Mr. John Barclay, would teach two children of 'decayed' guild brethren for nothing.[18] There was unanimous agreement to encourage George Mark, a professor of maths and bookkeeping, to teach in a public school by paying him £5 sterling a year, from Whitsunday 1743.[19] In 1785 the town council's plan to build a new academy, the utility of which it was said 'must be evident to all the Gentlemen present', evoked an annual contribution for three years of £20 sterling.[20]

Some years later, a schoolmaster, Francis Sievwright, who had suffered a loss of salary when the English and writing schools were divided, applied for redress from the Guildry, which he obtained.[21] He claimed that the new master was teaching his subjects and enticing pupils away from his establishment. In 1828 one member disapproved of their taking any notice of a report on the public seminaries on the ground that these were not in the hands of the inhabitants, but he got no support.[22] They approved changing the application of John Morgan's legacy to building a school instead of a hospital for 100 boys. They gave a testimonial to George Duncan, one of their members who had provided £1,200 to build an industrial school in the town, and attended the laying of the foundation stone in 1855.[23] The interest in education continues to the present day and the dean and one of his assessors are directors of the High School of Dundee.[24]

The amenities of the town were always a consideration. For instance when a complaint reached them about a soap-and-candlemaker setting up his malodorous business near a house, the petitioner was informed that such manufactures were strictly forbidden near the heart of a royal burgh. The offender and his insurers were faced with a petition and a visitation.[25] The condition of the streets was another matter which often appeared in the records. In November 1767, the town council consulted the Guildry and the Nine Trades, as financial assistance was needed to make any improvement. The council was prepared to pay £100 sterling out of the community's funds. A meeting in 1768, the exact date illegible because of water or fire damage, of Trades, Guildry and a council committee which had examined the town's accounts, agreed that that was all the town could afford for seven years. The sum of £2,000 was thought to be necessary and it was agreed that subscriptions should be asked for, each giving what they thought proper.[26] In 1832 the trustees of the Harbour Board and the council were each asked for £800 or 'such other sum as they think appropriate' for improving the paving.[27]

Another matter in which the Guildry had strong opinions, as did most of the population of the town, was the water supply. The water came from wells, which became totally inadequate as the number of inhabitants grew. When mills and, in the eighteenth century, increasing industrial development needed a constant and larger flow of water, the problem intensified. One firm, John Wemyss and Son, was accused by other users of causing the shortage in a Seagate well by 'improper conduct' – in other words making arrangements to obtain more water than the council had permitted.[28] In the 1780s the need for more water was stressed by manufacturers but with a council short of cash little was done. In the nineteenth century Dundee well water was admired for its sparkling appearance and delightful taste but unfortunately when it was analysed the origin of all these attractive characteristics turned out to be decomposed sewage.

In the 1830s the town council had decided to take action. Such were the strong feelings on the subject that 160 members of the Guildry met at a meeting in one of the churches to discuss the council's suggestion that inhabitants should be assessed to obtain a better supply.[29] The motion proposed at the meeting expressed disapproval of this in principle, as many people had already paid for a water supply and objected to paying for others, except for confessed paupers. An amendment proposing that the town should become responsible for providing sufficient water, funding it through assessment, was lost. The Guildry also protested against the council spending public money to oppose the act sought by a Joint Stock company which hoped to take over the task of supplying water. This all ended in tears. The company eventually became bankrupt, while the water supply remained inadequate and contaminated. The Guildry also regretted the haste with which the council had gone to parliament for a bill to enable water to be taken from the river Isla.

Few municipalities took on the responsibility for their burgh's water supply at that stage in Scotland and it was not until the 1860s that real improvement became possible. By that time the attitude of the majority had completely changed. The Guildry was then firmly of the opinion that water should be in the town's hands and a water rate was accepted almost as a matter of course. At a meeting of the dean and assessors in 1871, the only dissenting note came from the water manager of the old company, John Duncan, who made an impassioned speech asking for reduction in the consumption of water by everyone.[30] But the dean supported taking water from Lintrathen and that source was eventually adopted.

Fishing did not get as much attention as might have been expected, but merchants were not fishermen though they might export their catch. A project for a fishery company was before them in 1700, but was only recommended with no practical help,[31] while in 1720 all that they seemed to do about the proposal for a fishery company by the Convention of Royal Burghs was to 'give it their thoughts'.[32] In the 1820s more interest was shown, when they went so far as to petition parliament for better regulation and preservation of the Tay salmon fishery, when there was some controversy over the methods used for catching the fish.[33]

After winning its independence from the council, the incorporation used its liberty to comment on almost every important development in the town. Even after the abolition of its privileges it remained an efficient agent by which its members could voice their views; these also reflected the changes in society and the reactions to these changes, both favourable and unfavourable. In the 1820s the need for more landwaiters (customs officers) to cope with the increased trade at the harbour evoked an approach to the Commissioners of Customs. Only two were stationed in the town and this caused considerable delay for merchants.[34] Pilotage of the Tay was another matter which concerned them in 1848, when it was suggested that parliament should be applied to for an act to regulate it, though details were to be left in the hands of the Harbour Trust.[35] The new lunatic asylum, to which they contributed £1,500 to speed up the building in 1819, the opening of Dundee Royal Infirmary, the building and the disaster of the first railway bridge over the Tay, the Dundee to Newtyle railway, the appearance of tramways in 1877, all merited suitable notice. In January and February 1845, the line of the new railway to be built from Dundee to Perth aroused great interest with the determination not to allow the destruction of the leisure amenities of the Magdalen Yard in particular, nor to inconvenience the harbour. A motion by Mr. Flowerdew that the railway 'be not sanctioned' however, was voted for only by him and his seconder.[36] The proposal that the British Association should meet in Dundee had an enthusiastic reception in 1863, and this was accompanied by an encomium on the town, noting its architectural interest and the beauty of its surroundings, as well as areas of economic interest including the local linen and jute manufactures, the Fife coal mines and agriculture.[37] The 1912 meeting of the Association was equally welcomed and applauded after the event as being very successful.

Then there was the mail. In 1763 the fact that the mail from Perth went by Coupar Angus was met with disapproval.[38] In 1824 various means of speeding correspondence from north to south were in their minds. It took eighty-one hours for letters from London to reach Aberdeen, but that included waits of eighteen hours at Edinburgh, six and a half at Dundee and six at York, mainly because of the time local offices closed.[39] One member, Mr. James Chalmers, a bookseller, had been responsible for preparing all the information which would have cut the time to forty-nine hours and this was eventually achieved, largely through his efforts.[40] Later in the century, in 1862, when the Post Office had moved from the town house to Meadow Road, the dean was asked to 'memorialise' the authorities to suggest a receiving house for mail, or even a pillar near the town house for letters, but for some reason the postmaster-general did not think this was expedient.[41]

During the struggle with the council the suggestion that total political reform was the eventual aim was refuted with some strength, but by the end of the 1820s attitudes had veered round to support for greater democracy in both burgh and parliamentary elections. Though the council had become perhaps more efficient and less authoritarian than in the Riddoch days, there were still doubts about it. Its behaviour over the disputed election of the dean in 1827, the resistance to changes in the monopoly of the gas supply – in which some councillors had an interest – and the matter of the harbour improvements, were among the controversies which revived interest in burgh reform. At the end of 1830 general disapproval of the existing parliamentary system was also expressed when Mr David Jobson even proposed a ballot on the matter. In March 1831 it was decided that a petition should be sent to parliament asking for reform,[42] and after the Reform Act was passed members enthusiastically joined in a huge procession to celebrate.[43] In 1834, an address thanking Earl Grey for his part in achieving this remarked on how this was of special benefit to Scotland where 'For ages, she had experienced the benumbing influence of a selfish, haughty, mock representation'.[44] In 1867 there were special meetings held to petition parliament for additional representation for Scotland and especially for a second member for Dundee, which by that time had a population of over 110,000.[45]

The Guildry after 1846 was still represented on various boards, serving the Harbour, the Gas, Water and Police commissions and it is clear that the dean was a figure of influence and importance, an obvious first choice when directors of public institutions were appointed. A trustee of the Morgan hospital, a director of the Orphan Institution and the Lunatic Asylum, a manager of Dundee Savings

Bank, a trustee or patron of many private trusts, set up by individuals in their wills, as well as a town councillor and head of the Dean of Guild Court, the dean in 1872 must still have been a busy man.[46] Many of these bodies existed until governmental action affected them, by the nationalisation of the public utilities, for instance, but the dean, styled Lord Dean since 1889, is still *ex officio* a member of various trusts, and indeed is officially the second citizen of Dundee.[47]

While the act of 1846 abolished exclusive privileges, the various bodies affected were not deprived of their property. With no need today for a poor fund for members, the Guildry mainly uses its funds to give scholarships and awards connected with town planning and architecture, and matters in which they have been involved in the burgh from at least the seventeenth century. The students studying architecture and town planning at the University of Dundee, for instance, are now beneficiaries of this tradition.[48]

Currently there are around two hundred members in the incorporation. New members apply for entrance with the support of established brethren and as in the past fees paid by their sons and sons-in-law are less than those with no family connections. Indeed, the category of life only membership also remains in place. The Guildry may no longer be a defender of exclusive privilege but the incorporation has undoubtedly retained its sense of civic responsibility and can also look back with some pride on its long history.

NOTES

[1] DCA; G1/6, 9-3-1831.
[2] DCA; G1/6, 18-11-1826.
[3] DCA; G1/6, 26-5-1841.
[4] DCA; G3/3, February 1832.
[5] DCA; G1/6, 3-4-1833.
[6] DCA; G1/6, 18-3-1833.
[7] DCA; G1/6, 1-4-1833.
[8] DCA; G1/7, 1842 accounts, audited 1844.

9   DCA; G3/3, *passim.*

10 DCA; G1/7, 6-8-1846, 25-8-1846.

11 DCA; G1/8.

12 DCA; G1/2, 30-6-1716.

13 DCA; G2/1, 29-11-1841.

14 DCA; G1/2, 16-3-1699.

15 DCA; G/2a, 16-3-1699.

16 DCA; G1/5, 19-4-1820.

17 DCA; G1/2, 8-5-1700.

18 DCA; G1/2, 7-6-1712, 22-10-1722.

19 DCA; TC56/2, 19-4-1743.

20 DCA; G1/4, 29-12-1785.

21 DCA; G1/4, 19-9-1793.

22 DCA; G1/6, 6a, 29-10-1828, 8-10-1828.

23 DCA; G2/1, 25-1-1852.

24 Goodfellow, v.

25 DCA; G1/4, 1779.

26 DCA; G1/4, 1767, 1768.

27 DCA; G1/6, 28-1-1833.

28 DCA; DTC, 10-11-1779.

29 DCA; G1/6, November 1834.

30 DCL; Lamb 195 (25).

31 DCA; G1/2, 8-8-1700.

32 DCA; G1/2, 21 May, 28 June, 1720.

33 DCA; G1/5, 13-3-1824, 10-4-1823,21-4-1827. See C.J. Davey, *The Last Toot; the end of salmon fishing in Broughty Ferry* (CETAFS Occasional Paper, 2, 1991).

34 DCA; G1/4, 17-4-1822, G1/5, 22-4-1822.

35 DCA; G1/7, 27-9-1848, 4-10-1848.

36 DCA; G1/7, 8, 21, January, 8, 20 February 1845.

37 DCA; G1/7, 28-7-1863.

38 DCA; TC56/2, 22-11-1763.

39 DCA; G1/5, 13-3-1824.

40 W. Norrie, *Dundee Celebrities of the Nineteenth Century* (Dundee, 1873), 152.

41 DCA; G1/7, 23-6-1862.

42 DCA; G1/6 December 1830, 9-3-1831. I have to thank Mr. I. Gilroy for allowing me to read his unpublished work 'Burgh Reform in Dundee 1815-1831' which illuminates the politics of this period. I must also thank Mr. Dennis Collins for bringing this work to my notice.

[43]   DCA; G1/6, 6-8-1832.

[44]   DCA; G1/6, 8-9-1834.

[45]   DCA; G1/8, 16-6-1867, 19-6-1867,G8/79, memo to Earl of Derby.

[46]   Warden, 225.

[47]   Information from Mr. D. Goodfellow and Mr. D. Collins

[48]   www.Dundee.ac.uk/pressreleases/prjun00/guildry.htm.

BIBLIOGRAPHY

Primary Sources

Manuscripts

Dundee Town Council Minutes
Records of Dundee Merchant Guild
Records of the Maltmen Incorporation of Dundee

Printed

Adam, W., *Vitruvius Scoticus* with notes by James Simpson (Edinburgh, 1980).

Grant, F.F. (ed.), *The Commissariot Record of Brechin* (SRS, Edinburgh, 1902).

Hay, W. (ed.), *Charters, Writs and Public Documents of the Royal Burgh of Dundee* (Dundee, 1880).

Innes, C., *Ancient Laws and Customs of the Burghs of Scotland*, i, 1124-1424 (S.B.R.S, 1868).

Marwick, J.D. (ed.), *Extracts from the Records of the Convention of the Royal Burghs of Scotland* (Edinburgh, 1866-1880).

Millar, A.H. (ed.), *The Compt Buik of David Wedderburne* (Scottish History Society, 1898).

Millar, A.H. (ed.), *Roll of Eminent Burgesses of Dundee*, 1513-1880 (Dundee, 1887).

Stavert, M.L. (ed.), *Perth Guildry Book*, 1452-1601 (SRS, no.19, Edinburgh, 1993).

Thomson, T. and Innes, C. (eds.), *The Acts of Parliament of Scotland*, 12 vols. (Edinburgh, 1815-1875).

Report of Commissioners on Municipal Corporations of Scotland (1835)

Secondary Sources

Anon. Review of C. Gross, *The Gild Merchant*, in *Scottish Review*, 32 (1989), 71.

Baxter, J.H., *Dundee and the Reformation* (Abertay Historical Society Publication, 7, Dundee, 1960).

Black, A., *Guilds and Civil Societies in European Political Thought from the Twelfth Century to the Present* (London, 1984).

Brown, M., *James I* (Edinburgh, 1994).

Campbell, R.H. and Skinner, A., *The Origins of the Scottish Enlightenment* (Edinburgh, 1982).

Connor, R.D., and Simpson, A.D.C., *Weights and Measures in Scotland, A European Perspective* (East Linton, 2004).

Ewan, E., *Town Life in Fourteenth Century Scotland* (Edinburgh, 1990).

Fry, M., *The Dundas Despotism* (Edinburgh, 1992).

Gauldie, E., *One Artful and Ambitious Individual, Alexander Riddoch, (1745-1819)* (Abertay Historical Society Publication, 28, Dundee 1989).

Grant, I.F., *Social and Economic Development of Scotland before 1603* (Edinburgh and London, 1930).

Goodfellow, D., *The Guildry of Dundee* (Dundee, 1997).

Gordon, G. and Dicks, B. (eds.), *Scottish Urban History* (Aberdeen, 1983).

Gray, I., *A Guide to Dean of Guild Court Records* (Glasgow, 1994).

Gross, C., *The Gild Merchant* (Oxford, 1890).

Houston, R.A. and Knox, W.W.J. (eds.), *The New Penguin History of Scotland* (Harmondsworth, 2001).

Houston, R.A. and Whyte, I.D. (eds.), *Scottish Society, 1500-1800* (Cambridge, 1989).

Jackson, A.M., *Glasgow Dean of Guild Court* (Glasgow, 1983).

Lenman, B., *From Esk to Tweed* (Glasgow, 1975).

Logue, K.J., *Popular Disturbances in Scotland, 1780-1815* (Edinburgh, 1979).

Lynch, M., Spearman, M., and Stell, G. (eds.), *The Scottish Medieval Town* (Edinburgh, 1988).

Lynch, M. (ed.), *The Oxford Companion to Scottish History* (Oxford, 2001).

Lynch, M. (ed.), *The Early Modern Town in Scotland* (London, 1987).

Mackenzie, W.M., *The Scottish Burghs* (Edinburgh, 1949).

Maxwell, A., *The History of Old Dundee* (Edinburgh and Dundee, 1884).

Maxwell, A., *Old Dundee, Prior to the Reformation* (Edinburgh and Dundee, 1891).

McNeill, P.G.B. and McQueen, H.L. (eds.), *Atlas of Scottish History to 1707* (Edinburgh, 1996).

McNeill, P.G.B. and Nicholson, R. (eds.), *An Historical Atlas of Scotland, c.400-c.1600* (St Andrews, 1975).

Miskell, L., Whatley, C.A. and Harris, B. (eds.), *Victorian Dundee: image and realities* (East Linton, 2000).

Morris, D.B., *The Stirling Merchant Gild and Life of John Cowane* (Stirling, 1919).

Murray, D., *Early Burgh Organization in Scotland*, 2 vols., (Glasgow, 1924-32).

Nicholas, D., *The Later Medieval City, 1300-1500* (London and New York, 1997).

Norrie, W., *Dundee Celebrities* (Dundee, 1878).

Riis, T., *Should Auld Acquaintance be Forgot* (Odense, 1988).

Scott, A.M., *Dundee's Literary Lives*, Vol. 1 (Abertay Historical society Publication no.42, Dundee, 2003).

Simpson, G.G. (ed.), *Scotland and the Low Countries* (East Linton, 1996).

Smith, A.M., *The Three United Trades of Dundee* (Abertay Historical Society Publication, no.26, Dundee, 1987).

Smith, A.M., *The Nine Trades of Dundee* (Abertay Historical Society Publications no.35, Dundee, 1995).

Stevenson, S. and Torrie, E.P.D., *Historic Dundee* (Scottish Burgh Survey, 1988).

Torrie, E.P.D. (ed.), *The Gild Court of Dunfermline* (S.R.S., New Series, 12).

Torrie, E.P.D., *Medieval Dundee* (Abertay Historical Society Publication no.30, Dundee, 1990).

Warden, A.J., *Burgh Laws of Dundee* (London, 1972).

Whatley, C.A., Swinfen, D.B. and Smith, A.M., *The Life and Times of Dundee* (Edinburgh, 1993).

Articles in Periodicals

Close, R., 'Planning and building records', in SLH, 39 (1997).

Gray, I., 'Dean of Guild Court Records: a unique source for Scottish urban history', in *Scottish Archives*, 5 (1999).

Tyson, R.E., 'Poverty and Relief', in *Scottish Archives*, 8 (2000).

Unpublished Work

Cowper, G., 'Guild Notices and Processes' (DCA, typescript).

Flett, I.E.F., 'The conflict of the Reformation and Democracy in the Geneva of Scotland' (MPhil thesis degree, St. Andrews University, 1981).

Gemmill, E., 'Trade Signs and Symbols', lecture at Scottish Medievalists conference, Pitlochry, 2000.

Gilroy, I.D., manuscript research on Dundee burgh politics in the early nineteenth century, n.d.

Wyllie, W., 'The Guildry Incorporation of Dundee', typescript in Dundee City Archive, n.d.

APPENDIX 1

NOTE ON COINAGE AND WEIGHTS.

NOTE ON COINAGE.

Scottish coins were not plentiful and there was no enthusiasm about letting them out of the country. Any sound foreign currency was acceptable, but there had to be agreement on their value. For instance, in 1676 a committee of the Convention of Royal Burghs presented their proposals on 'bringing in foreign coinage', giving them an intrinsic value and 'for keeping our own coinage within this kingdom'. Among a long list, Spanish and Dutch ducats were to be worth £3 10s Scots; a piece of eight, weighing fourteen drops equalled £2 17s; a French crown £2 16s; a quadruple Spanish pistol weighing fourteen drops, £42 Scots. The Scots also used the merk (anglicé mark) which was worth 13s 4d.

All sums of money are given in the text as they appeared in the original documents. Until decimalisation, sterling consisted of pounds, shillings and pence and was expressed as £ s d. The relative values were twelve pennies (12d) to the shilling (1s) and twenty shillings to the pound. There were also halfpennies (bawbees) and farthings, worth one quarter of a penny. It should also be noted that during the later medieval and early modern periods, the Scots pound gradually lost its value compared to the pound sterling and, from 1603, was usually reckoned as worth one-twelfth of the pound sterling. After 1707 sterling became the currency throughout Great Britain, although records continued to be kept using notional Scottish money.

SCOTTISH WEIGHTS

Scottish weights varied from time to time, from one burgh to another and for different types of goods. Continental measures were also used. For those who would like to understand them fully, a new book, of only 841 pages, which has recently been published, repays consultation. This is *Weights and Measures in Scotland, A European Perspective* by R.D. Connor and A.D.C. Simpson, edited by A.D. Morrison-Low.

APPENDIX 2

LIST OF OFFICE-BEARERS AND MEMBERS OF THE
GUILDRY INCORPORATION
(at 31st December 2004)

Lord Dean of Guild: Alexander Murdoch

Assessors:
Scott Carswell Henderson   Lord Dean 1990-1993
David Goodfellow   Lord Dean 1996-1999
Sinclair Aitken   Lord Dean 1999-2003
Edward Hunter Leslie Shepherd
John Greig Sibbald
Dennis Ferguson Collins
Stuart Ross Leslie Shepherd
Michael Robert Forman Clark
James Iain Merry
Richard Scott Henderson
Graeme Wilson Spowart
Robert William Burns
George Brian Robertson Cram
David Stevenson Adam
John Stewart Robertson
David Anderson Comb
William Neil Cuthbert
Charles Fraser Scott Williamson

Clerk:	Michael Robert Forman Clark
Deputy Clerk:	Charles Fraser Scott Williamson
Collector:	Alexander John Cameron
Archivist:	Dennis Ferguson Collins
Chaplain:	Rev. Keith Ferrier Hall
Officer:	Gordon Williamson
Keeper of the Gavel:	Bruce Allan Kelly

APPENDIX 3

LIST OF MEMBERS OF THE GUILDRY INCORPORATION
(at 31st December 2004)

David Stevenson Adam
David Miller Aitken
Innes Alexander Aitken
Rhogan Iain Mackenzie Aitken
Sinclair Aitken
John Prophet Allardice
George Boyd Balrd
Robert Hall Barnett
Normile Edward Alexander George
  Wyndham Elliot Baxter
William Stewart Baxter
Robert James Baxter
Robin Edward Elliot Baxter
Alastair William Elliot Baxter
Angus Normile Elliot Baxter
Richard Bishop
Richard Mercer Blaikie
Angus MacDonald Bowman
Bernard Neil Bowman
Leslie Alexander Bowman
James Ritchie Bowman
Alistair Robert Duff Bowman
Dr. Oswald Taylor Brown
Ewan Stewart Douglas Bruce
Roger McEwan Bruce
Robert Douglas Bruce
Prof. Stewart Brymer
Richard Stephen Burnett
Robert William Burns

Alexander John Cameron
Capt. Simon Douglas Robert
  Campbell
Ian Henry Buist Carmichael
Nigel Cayzer
Sir James Cayzer, Bart.
Alasdair David Chalmers
Robert Phillip Clark
Michael Robert Forman Clark
Richard Phillip Harley Clark
John Richard Clarke
Dennis Ferguson Collins
Rev. Ross Nicoll Ferguson Collins
David Anderson Comb
James William Coull
Neil Alexander Coupar
Alexander Coupar
David Thomas Murray Craig
Stewart Colville Cram
George Brian Robertson Cram
George Brown Cram
David Crawford
William Neil Cuthbert
Harry Dickson
Capt. Ramsay Dinnie
Alastair Gordon Drummond
George Gordon Drummond
William Andrew Soutar Dryden
Innes Alfred Duffiis
Eric David Duncan

Alan Michael Duncan
Dr. Ian Douglas Duncan
Robert Dunn
Alan Blyth Findlay
William Knight Fitzgerald
Robert Lang Fleming
Iain Ernest Farquhar Flett
Ian Graham Fraser
James Andrew Gellatly
Paul Nicholas Gletnak
Alister David Inglis Goodfellow
David Goodfellow
Ian Hamilton Goodfellow
Andrew Alister Goodfellow
Martin Nicholas Goodfellow
David William Scott Goodfellow
Donald Neil Gordon
Donald Blane Grant
Lovat Grant
John Aimer Grieve
John Stewart Grieve
Ronald Stewart Boyd Grieve
James Colin Garforth Halley
Sir Douglas Fleming Hardie
James Michael Hardie
Richard Scott Henderson
Scott Carswell Henderson
Stephen Matthew Henderson
Frederick George Allison Hibberd
James Alexander Inverarity
Bruce William McLaren Johnston
Dr. David Andrew Johnston
Allan Keillor
William John Keillor
Capt Arthur Edwin Kerr
Neil Prophet Key

George Balharrie Kinnes
John David Kyd
William Binnie Kydd
Alasdair Reid Moncrieff Laurie
Lord Provost John Ross Letford
Matthew James Little
James George Lockhart
William Barclay Low
Peter Soutar Low
Eric Crichton Lowson
Archibald MacNab
David Laing Macpherson
Michael McDonald
Angus McDonald
John Morrison McGregor
Brian John Cregan McKernie
Dr. James Paton McPherson
Michael Robert McWilliam
Thomas Alistair Ireland Martin
George Kemlo Martin
Jacob Matheson
Chessor Lille Matthew
John Kelman Mearns
Donald Edward Meekison
James Iain Merry
Ian Robert Milne
Angus McArthur Milton
Grant Melville Mitchell
David Melville Henderson Mitchell
Alexander Murdoch
Alexander Graham Murdoch
Ian Pulsford Murray
Robert Nimmo
Ewan Thomas Pate
David Kinross Paton
James Kinross Paton

James William Graham Patrick
Murray Petrie
Cmdr. John Douglas Picton
Gordon Stanley Pool
David Howard Price
Simon Roger Pritchard
John Stewart Pritchard
Ian Bell Rae
Christopher William Wallace Rea
David Baird Reid
Gordon Roderick Reid
Donald Thomas Ridgeway
George Fraser Ritchie
John Stewart Robertson
Mervyn James Rolfe
The Rt. Hon. Lord Ross (Donald
    MacArthur Ross)
Prof. William Lockerby Russell
Alexander George Scott
Gerald John Sharp
Derek Herbert James Shaw
Stuart Ross Leslie Shepherd
Alfred Kingsley Leslie Shepherd
Scott Buchan Leslie Shepherd
Edward Hunter Leslie Shepherd
Joseph Leslie Shepherd
John Greig Sibbald
Gavin James Greig Sibbald
David Greig Sibbald
Iain Greig Sibbald
John Smith Sibbald
David Robert Smith
Andrew Harvey Smith
Alexander Smith
Graeme Wilson Spowart
Jonathan Stewart
Adrian Arthur MacGregor Stewart

Alexander Watson Stiven
Prof. George Alexander Stout
Ian William Guthrie Sturrock
Gavin Robert Suggett
Alastair Summers
John Summers
Dr. Graham Summers
Dr. Ronald Summers
Aubrey Summers
Dr. Ronald Watson Summers
Brian Summers
Alastair John Duncan Taylor
Andrew Douglas Ross Taylor
Brig. Iain Scott Taylor
Donald Rutherford Taylor
Harry Terrell
Graham Thomson
Duncan McKenzie Torbet
Capt. Norman Tuddenham
David Hamilton Tweedie
Richard von Hoven
James McHardy Wallace
John Alan Smith Weatherhead
The Very Rev. Dr. James Leslie
    Weatherhead
Keith Williamson
Charles Fraser Scott Williamson
Gordon Williamson
George Willsher
Guy Douglas Wilson
Michael John Wilson
Gavin Garnet Wilson
William Gordon Withers
Kenneth Harry Wood
James Harvey Rutherford Wright
Iain Ritchie Young
Dennis James Young

APPENDIX 4

LIST OF THE DEANS OF GUILD OF DUNDEE FROM 1868 AND LORD DEANS OF GUILD OF DUNDEE FROM 1889
(Note: Warden lists the Deans from 1554 to 1870)

1868-1873	Robert McNaughtan, Hotel Keeper
1873-1877	James Luke, Merchant
1877-1881	Charles Edward, Architect
1881-1884	Alexander Henderson, Flaxspinner
1884-1888	Alexander Mathewson, Tea Merchant
1888-1892	Henry McGrady, Merchant
1892-1894	James Luke, Merchant
1894-1897	George Brodie Paul, Solicitor
1897-1900	William Brown Robertson, Grocer
1900-1903	James Bell, Timber Merchant
1903-1905	Thomas Lyle Peters, Commission Merchant
1905-1908	David Dickie, Wholesale Ironmonger
1908-1912	Thomas Dall Smibert, Master Baker
1912-1914	Peter Strachan Nicoll, Colliery and Shipping Agent
1914-1919	David Dickie, Wholesale Ironmonger
1919-1920	Peter Strachan Nicoll, Colliery and Shipping Agent
1920-1923	Thomas Milne, Builder
1923-1926	Christopher Johnston Bissett, Sheriff Clerk
1926-1929	Simon Forrest, Shipbroker
1929-1935	William Halley Brown, Brewer
1935-1938	Charles Hay Marshall, Solicitor
1938-1944	William Clark, Master Butcher
1944-1947	Alexander Lickley Proctor, Property Agent
1947-1950	James Strachan Nicoll, Colliery and Shipping Agent
1950-1954	William Steven Goodfellow, Master Baker

1954-1960	Thomas Rattray Murray, Property Agent
1960-1966	Alexander Smart Drummond, Master Painter
1966-1969	Andrew Wallace, Master Baker
1969-1975	Alexander Eric Larg, Music Seller
1975-1978	Thomas Hill Thoms, Architect
1978-1984	Gerald Alexander Burnett, Chartered Surveyor
1984-1987	William Wallace Rea, Banker
1987-1990	Bernard Neil Bowman, Solicitor
1990-1993	Scott Carswell Henderson, Jeweller and Silversmith
1993-1996	Ronald Stewart Boyd Grieve, Accountant
1996-1999	David Goodfellow, Master Baker
1999-2003	Sinclair Aitken, Haulage Contractor
2003-	Alexander Murdoch, Wholesale and Retail Grocer

INDEX OF PEOPLE

INDEX OF PLACE NAMES
OUTWITH DUNDEE

GENERAL INDEX

The Abertay Historical Society

Honorary Presidents
Lord Provost of the City of Dundee
Principal of the University of Dundee
Principal of the University of St Andrews

President
Steve Connelly

Vice-President
Frances Grieve

General Secretary
Matthew Jarron
c/o University of Dundee Museum Services, Dundee DD1 4HN
e-mail: museum@dundee.ac.uk

Treasurer
Charlotte Lythe
90 Dundee Road, Broughty Ferry, Dundee DD5 1DW
e-mail: c.lythe1@btinternet.com

Book Editors
Dr W Kenefick & Dr A MacDonald
Department of History, University of Dundee, Dundee DD1 4HN

Sales Secretary
Catherine Smith
SUAT, 55 South Methven Street, Perth PH1 5NX
e-mail: csmith@suat.demon.co.uk

The Society was founded in May 1947 and exists to promote interest in local history. For further information, please visit our website at www.abertay.org.uk

Publications of the Abertay Historical Society currently in print

No.27   Kenneth J. Cameron, *The Schoolmaster Engineer,*
         Adam Anderson of Perth and St Andrews c.1780-1846. (1988)
         ISBN 0 900019 23 9

No.28   *Enid Gauldie, One Artful and Ambitious Individual, Alexander*
         Riddoch (1745-1822), (Provost of Dundee 1787-1819). (1989)
         ISBN 0 900019 24 7

No.34   Ian McCraw, *The Fairs of Dundee.* (1994) ISBN 0 90019 30 1

No.35   Annette M. Smith, *The Nine Trades of Dundee.* (1995)
         ISBN 0 900019 31 X

No.36   Sylvia Robertson and Patricia Young, *Daughter of Atholl,*
         Lady Evelyn Stewart Murray, 1868-1940. (1996)
         ISBN 0 900019 32 8

No.37   Michael St John, *The Demands of the People, Dundee*
         Radicalism 1850-1870. (1997) ISBN 0 900019 33 6

No.38   W.M. Mathew, *Keiller's of Dundee, The Rise of the Marmalade*
         Dynasty 1800-1879. (1998) ISBN 0 900019 35 2

No.39   Lorraine Walsh, *Patrons, Poverty & profit: Organised Charity*
         in Nineteenth Century Dundee. (2000) ISBN 0 900019 35 2

No.40   Stewart Howe, *William Low & Co., A Family Business*
         History. (2000) ISBN 0 900019 36 0

No.41   Ian McCraw, *Victorian Dundee at Worship.* (2002)
         ISBN 0 900019 37 9

No.42   Andrew Murray Scott, *Dundee's Literary Lives vol 1: Fifteenth to Nineteenth Century.* (2003) ISBN 0 900019 38 7

No 43   Andrew Murray Scott, *Dundee's Literary Lives vol 2: Twentieth Century.* (2004) ISBN 0 900019 39 5

No 44   Claire Swan, *Scottish Cowboys and the Dundee Investors* (2005) ISBN 0 900019 40 9

All publications may be obtained through booksellers or by post from the Hon Sales Secretary, Abertay Historical Society, SUAT, 55 South Methven Street, Perth, PH1 5NX (e-mail: csmith@suat.demon.co.uk)